Against a I

AGAINST A FEDERAL EUROPE

The Battle for Britain

William Cash, MP

Duckworth

First published in 1991 by
Gerald Duckworth & Co. Ltd.
The Old Piano Factory
48 Hoxton Square, London N1 6PB

A catalogue record for this book is available from the British Library

ISBN 0 7156 2398 2

Printed in Great Britain by
Redwood Press Ltd., Melksham

Contents

Prologue

> We know that we have made no discoveries, and we believe that no discoveries are to be made, in morality, nor in the idea of liberty, nor many of the great principles of government which were understood long before we were born...In England...we have not been drawn and trussed in order that we may be filled, like stuffed birds, with chaff and rags and paitry blurred sheets of paper about the rights of man.
>
> Edmund Burke, *Reflections on the Revolution in France.*

Federalism is looming over Europe. Britain must decide whether or not it is willing to sign amendments to the Treaty of Rome which would pave its way and would effectively mean the end of Westminster democracy. Britain could become a mere province in a Europe dominated by Germany. This requires deeper and more open examination than it has so far received. The original aim of the European Community, to contain Germany within a legal supranational structure, has failed because Germany's success has given her disproportionate influence, even power, over its decision making. This is not the fault of Germany. It may be no one's fault but the consequences are considerable.

This book argues that Britain must not be pushed into accepting, nor accept, what cannot be in its interests. The United Kingdom may have faults but its democratic tradition is not one of them. Westminster must remain the effective Parliament of this proud and historic nation. Without democracy there can be no lasting economic prosperity. This applies throughout Europe. Britain may have much to learn about price stability and economic growth from its partners in Europe, but this is no reason for us to go along with federalism. The federalists would demolish the democratic institutions of Europe's nations in their drive to build a European Federation, just as the USSR and Eastern Europe are moving the other way. Nationalism combined with effective and accountable democracy within Europe should be encouraged, as the author argued in 'A Democratic Way to European Unity – Arguments Against Federalism' (The Bow Group, June 1990).

The federalists' 'Europeanism' is a dangerous nationalism writ large over Europe which seeks to dominate countries and continents. It would produce rival economic blocs in the Far East and in North America. International trade and peace would suffer. The emergence of a sclerotic dirigiste EC based on a centralised over-powerful Brussels bureaucracy will rob Europe of the essence of economic success, which is genuine democracy. It would institutionalise Germany's domination of Europe rather than contain it.

The British electorate must ask: do we want to enter an irreversible union in which the will of the British people could consistently be overridden on vital matters such as the allocation of public expenditure, including defence? Without proper information they cannot ask, let alone answer, that question. This book seeks to redress some of the balance.

Preface

My first involvement with European politics was shortly after coming down from Oxford when I visited the European Coal and Steel Community offices in the mid-1960s. It seemed clear at the time that Britain was set on entering the European Community despite the objections of President de Gaulle. I wrote a paper for the Bow Group on steel denationalisation and the European Coal and Steel Community.

I have always been a supporter of moves to greater co-operation in Europe, but not at the expense of our national sovereignty in fundamental areas of government. In the 1975 referendum I voted to remain in the European Community and went on to help found the Westminster for Europe group.

Shortly after my election as Member of Parliament for Stafford in 1984, I was appointed to the Select Committee on European Legislation. It was then that I realised what was really going on: the European Community was in danger of rapidly becoming a political federation although this was always denied. The issue of Europe at this time did not figure highly in the minds of many. My interest was spurred on by a visit the Select Committee made to Brussels at the end of 1985 prior to the Single European Act. I was disturbed by the number of officials I met from the European Commission whose federalism was beyond doubt.

At the suggestion of George Brock of *The Times*, I wrote an article on the Single European Act in 1986. It was the first of a series of articles I was to write for *The Times* over the next four years warning of 'creeping federalism'.

During this period I expressed my growing concern in letters and memoranda to the Prime Minister and raised the matter on the floor of the House. I tabled an amendment to the Single European Act that 'nothing in this Act shall derogate from the sovereignty of the United Kingdom Parliament'. If I accepted that the advantages of a limited extension of majority voting outweighed its disadvantages, I was adamant that it should be reaffirmed where real power and sovereignty lay – with the British people.

By October 1988 when I attended a Berlin conference on European Union organised by the European Peoples Party in the Reichstag, it was clear that the thrust for federalism in Europe was gathering pace. Here the determination to establish a European political union with a single government and a single parliament was quite breathtaking. It was clear that federalism was on the move. The goal of a single European market was being hijacked by Euro-crusaders intent on knocking twelve European nations into one super-Euro state.

Following the Bruges speech by the then Prime Minister, Mrs Margaret Thatcher, on 18 September 1988, a number of colleagues and I formed the Friends of Bruges in the House as an informal grouping of MPs to promote the anti-federalist message of the Bruges speech inside Parliament. I did not become a member of the Bruges Group itself. At the end of 1989 we were elected officers of the Conservative Backbench Committee on European Affairs. This demonstrated the level of concern felt within the party about the direction in which the EC was heading. This was borne out by our re-election after Mrs Thatcher's resignation in November 1990.

I was then appointed to Douglas Hurd's Manifesto Committee and invited by him to write the paper on the future of Britain and Europe. Shortly afterwards I was asked to become a Parliamentary Private Secretary in the Foreign and Commonwealth Office, an offer I declined as it would have prevented me from voicing my growing concern about the federalist turn the EC was taking. With the launch of two Intergovernmental Conferences in December 1990 designed to pave the way for Economic, Monetary and Political Union, my greatest fears were rapidly being realised. I had warned, in my Bow Group pamphlet ('A Democratic Way to European Unity: Arguments Against Federalism', published in June 1990), that the federalists would force the pace and that Germany would dominate the new structure and Europe as a whole. The speed was staggering.

Once the Conferences were underway, it became a matter of increasing concern that information must be made available to MPs. If Parliament is to function properly, it needs to be kept fully informed, especially on an issue which so directly affects Westminster itself. It was only after intense lobbying that documents such as the Central Bank Statutes, the initial draft Treaties and proposals of the Commission were made available to the House of Commons.

It is, of course, understandable that the government must retain its negotiating position, but the reluctance to make information available on a matter of such vital importance to the future of Parliament and its democracy generated a sense of misgiving. It can only be helpful, if the the Government is to maintain the integrity of the United Kingdom

Parliament and its democratic traditions, that it should have the full and informed support of Parliament and the public.

Those of us who oppose the federalist tendencies of other member states and the Community institutions have been dismayed by the vast resources with which the federalist cause has been propagated; we have had little to fall back on, other than our comparatively slender means. I have been greatly encouraged by the support I have had from colleagues and members of the European Affairs Committee and from the votes of members of the public in debates throughout the country on this subject. I was particularly glad that on one occasion at the Oxford Union in May 1990 the defeated opponent was Edward Heath.

I want in particular to thank John Laughland for his tremendous help in research and in his contribution to the arguments, and also Jeremy Bradshaw for his help and steady flow of information. Wendy Ogilvie, my secretary, has as ever been patient and thorough. To my wife Biddy and family, William, Sam and Letitia, I owe a special word of thanks for putting up with me and with the mountain of paper which all this has generated.

Writing this in our home, which was once owned by the Ambassador to Hanover, Berlin and Copenhagen in the late 1690s during the negotiations for the Act of Succession, I cannot help wondering what he would have made of all this now. After all, it was the enforced abdication of James II which had saved our infant parliamentary democracy from the absolutist tendencies of the Stuarts. Let us hope that, at the conclusion of this process in the 1990s, we will not have gone full circle.

Upton Cressett William Cash
23 October 1991

1

Britain for Europe

England has saved herself by her exertions, and will, as I trust, save Europe by her example.

William Pitt, Guildhall, 1805.

The serious threat to our democracy is not the existence of foreign totalitarian states. It is the existence within our own personal attitudes and within our own institutions of conditions which have given a victory to external authority, discipline, uniformity and dependence upon The Leader in foreign countries. The battlefield is accordingly here – within ourselves – and our institutions.

John Dewey, *Freedom and Culture.*

Britain is and will always remain in Europe. No one who has a glimmering of British history can deny that Britain has played a major role in European affairs for centuries. In war and in peace, by marriage and by conquest, through the tenure of the Crown by the Normans who first settled here, and later by their control of French and Burgundian lands, through the accession to the throne of the Dutch William of Orange, and later the Hanoverian succession, through our alliances with nations throughout Europe, our engagement in war for the freedom of the continent, and now through our membership of the European Community, the British Crown and British history have long been deeply involved in Europe. It is extraordinary that Britain should now be accused of being isolationist and insular.

It is clear, however, that our island story has left us with a richer democratic inheritance than elsewhere on the continent. The depth of our parliamentary tradition and the accountability and procedures which go with it are of immense value to Britain and Europe, and have been widely influential throughout the world. Now, however, our democratic tradition, our greatest national asset, is under threat from the largely unseen and unread proposals before the Intergovernmental Conferences on political and economic union.

Since the 1950s, the European Community has sought to provide stability by balancing competing interests in a novel legal and economic structure. To do so it has relied heavily on the habit of inter-governmental co-operation and not the coercion of supranationalism. By respecting the integrity of differing nations, identities of interest have developed and areas of difference have been reduced. It has encouraged a balance of interests within a legal and economic framework and led to the 'habits of co-operation' described by the Foreign Secretary, Douglas Hurd. This has much to commend it. Unfortunately, political union is not the natural extension of these habits into other fields, as some like to pretend. On the contrary, it is a radical new departure, which, far from removing tensions between the various states, will exacerbate them, as it is based on the denial of national interest.

Furthermore, it will also destroy democratic accountability. The plan to give a decisive say in economic policy-making, including power to decide on public expenditure, to central bankers who would be constitutionally immune from democratic accountability, and thus to draw together twelve or more member states into one centralised economic and political system, would deprive the European Community of the political and democratic oxygen that it needs in order to develop along stable lines. If a country does not have the power to decide its economic priorities, then its parliament is a mere charade. A member of the French National Assembly said to the author recently, 'You fight for your Westminster democracy. If you lose it we all do.'

Democracy depends on the ability to hold decision-makers to account. A parliament must effectively scrutinise legislation, protect and represent the rights and interests of individuals, and connect government with the governed. Elections alone are not enough. If rigorous parliamentary procedures are abandoned and submerged in the fudge of federalism, power will slip away from the democratic arena into the hands of the most powerful.

Moreover, although economic forces and circumstances have a profound impact upon political life, if the political and democratic values and procedures for real accountability are not pre-eminent, as is the case in the United Kingdom and the United States, then no amount of economic integration will produce stability and prosperity. If any one lesson has to be learned from the dramatic developments in Eastern Europe and the USSR in the late 1980s and early 1990s, it is the fact that democracy is the crucial bedrock on which economic stability has to be founded. The primacy of democratic politics, the rule of law and parliamentary government over economic management must be preserved.

Nor do paper constitutions always reflect the realities of power, and propaganda about a 'Community' or 'federalism' is just talk. While the proposed central bank is to be 'independent', it is clear that the Germans will not accept it unless it suits them, and unless they can be sure that it will serve their interests. A tightly integrated political and economic framework in the EC would inevitably be decisively influenced by the country with the greatest economic weight, Germany. Majority voting in the Council of Ministers would mean that countries which are economically dependent on her would augment her power even further. This is especially true if a two-speed approach to EMU is adopted: it would simply mean that Germany's smaller neighbours would agree to annex themselves to the Deutsche-Mark/ecu zone. Thus a powerful core of countries would go ahead with its own plans, imposing conditions on the others, and negating the whole concept of a community. The French pretence that they can 'contain' Germany by imposing supranational Community control on her is looking increasingly dated, as Germany consolidates her position as the world's largest trading nation and can expect to have a GNP of $2-$3 trillion within the next eight or nine years. If there is now a drift to German economic and political domination, which is what the founders of the Community, Schuman and Monnet, most feared, then it can only be fairly countered by having a genuine single market and Community structures which are truly democratic.

Above all, one has to ask, what is this all for? There is no point in creating a European Union unless its aims are clear: it would be like a character in search of an author in the Theatre of the Absurd. One would have to be blind, or worse, not to see that Europe has changed since the Berlin Wall came down, and now that the Soviet Union has collapsed. Why seek to put new wine into old bottles by reinforcing European Community structures which date from the 1950s, and whose origins lie in the Cold War? Anyone can see that the imperative now is to create a wider Europe, bringing in the nascent democracies of the East. At the same time, the more countries there are in the Community, the more difficult it will be to reach agreement together. The conclusion is surely not to reinforce a central core of rich countries who will impose their will on the rest, but rather to recognise that the scope for centralised co-operation and control in fundamental policy areas, such as economic, foreign and defence policy, simply has its limits, especially when there is no common enemy any more against whom to unite. We must be realistic in our aims: a European Union should not be an end in itself.

It is no coincidence that it is primarily in Britain that these questions are being raised even if the level of information is less than required. British people, accustomed to an exceptionally high level of political debate in the press and parliament, would be very mistaken to think that the European issue is being debated in the same way by our European partners: it is not. French, German, Italian and other voters are going into this with their eyes shut. The real accountability and transparency of our democratic system, perhaps best exemplified by the rigorous cross-examination of ministers in Select Committees, or by the famous institution of Prime Minister's Questions (an ordeal very few other Premiers in the world have to face) serve as a model for other member states. This is also true where scrutiny of European Community legislation coming out of Brussels is concerned. We have recently established new Standing Committees for the purpose, which is a step in the right direction. If we have much to learn from others about anti-inflationary policies, so too do other member states have much to learn from us about our democratic traditions and political culture. The current proposals put before the Intergovernmental Conferences, particularly those on monetary and political union, would damage not only British democracy, but democracy in Europe as a whole.

Britain and its democracy in Westminster played an absolutely fundamental role in the Second World War in saving Europe from German hegemony and dictatorship, a matter which it is scarcely thought decent to mention these days, but during and immediately after the war, Winston Churchill repeatedly called for a rapprochement between the nations of Europe. Far from being isolated from Europe, Winston Churchill and the British government were continuously making constructive suggestions as to the way in which Europe could proceed. This was most famously exemplified by his speech in Zurich in 1946. However, as he was only too well aware, there was a substantial difference between the democratic tradition of Britain and that of its continental neighbours. Moreover, although in the Zurich speech he refers to a 'kind of United States of Europe', it is clear that he did not see Britain being limited to a purely European role: his 'three circles' emphasised Britain's relations with the US and the Commonwealth as well. In 1953, the same year as the failure of the European Defence Community, he explicitly rejected the idea of British entanglement in a European federal system.[1]

In the meantime, Robert Schuman, born of German parents but having become a French national in 1919 and with his background of resistance to the German occupation, had sought an answer to 'the German question'. Just as at this time Britain was preoccupied with disengagement from the Empire, so France and Germany became properly preoccupied with one another and with a determination not to have another world war. Robert Schuman argued that France would have to take the initiative if she was to avoid having a British-American plan imposed on the embryonic EC.[2] Schuman felt that the Council of Europe, created in May 1949, was incapable of achieving the French aim of binding Germany in, since it left member states entirely sovereign. He decided to set up his project on the basis of a Franco-German axis within a European framework, initially limited to coal and steel under the jurisdiction of a supranational authority, convinced that supranationalism was the only way to contain Germany. Like all French policy-makers since, including de Gaulle, Mitterrand and Delors, Schuman and Jean Monnet were motivated by one overriding concern: to prevent Germany's domination. In a note dated 3 May 1950, Jean Monnet wrote that Schuman intended that, 'with the solution proposed, the question of the domination of the German industry would disappear, the existence of which would create fear in Europe, cause constant troubles, finally impede the European Union and cause again the loss of Germany itself. This solution would, on the contrary, create for the German, as well as the French and the European industry, the conditions of common expansion and competition but without domination'.[3] Nothing could be more ironic, as later chapters show. Jean Monnet also insisted that there could be no European Community without Britain.

Much criticism has been levelled at Britain for her attitude to the European Community when it was founded. It is suggested that she was stand-offish and reluctant to participate. It was hardly surprising that, during the period of disengagement from the Empire and the development of the Commonwealth, she would need to 'find a role', nor that, as a world power with her own nuclear forces and a seat in the United Nations Security Council, Britain's foreign policy priorities were not limited to the confines of Europe. Nevertheless, as so often in the past, her contribution to Europe is not in doubt. Britain had imposed rationing to help the starving German people and even gave Germany 25% of her Marshall Aid, some of which is still part of a capital fund making cheap loans available to German industry. The special relationship between Britain and America, cemented during the war, was the lynchpin of NATO when it was established in 1949. This had as its raison d'être the defence of Western Europe. The Western European Union was established in 1954, prompted by American pressure following the abandonment of the European Defence Community, which the French had rejected because of its supranational character. The WEU Treaty emphasised national interests within the framework of European co-operation, and Britain agreed to maintain a strong continental presence with four divisions and an air presence in West Germany. Eden abandoned our age-old policy of avoiding a permanent military commitment in Europe in order to assuage French concern about Germany. Even though Suez led Macmillan to focus on a special relationship with President Eisenhower in 1957, the British commitment to the Western European Union was increased in the same year to meet rising costs. In 1963 Harold Macmillan applied to join the European Community, a mere six years after the Community itself was born in 1957.

It is unfortunate that, just as the 'winds of change' were blowing away Britain's colonial heritage, she encountered a breezy response from General de Gaulle, Churchill's protégé, who, obsessed with resisting the Anglo-Saxons to whom his country owed her very freedom, twice vetoed her application to join the Community (in 1963 and 1968). Thus it can hardly be said that Britain was in any way standing aloof from Europe, but was fully engaged in seeking to play her part in the evolving political and economic situation on the continent, as was shown by her subsequent initiative in setting up the European Free Trade Area, which on 22 October 1991 made an economic agreement with the Community which represents an important step in relation to the single market.

The continuing attempts to bridge the Europe/Atlantic relationship were reinforced by the British offer in 1964 to draw the West Germans into an 'Atlantic nuclear force' with the British Polaris fleet. The following year the Labour government embarked on a Franco-British aircraft system and in 1967 Harold Wilson made a further application for Britain to join the European Community. Eventually the Heath government took Britain into the European Community in 1973. The iniquitous terms on which we entered, together with the Labour Party's schizophrenic attitude to membership led to more than a decade of bad odour between Britain and the Community. Unfortunately, as soon as the budget scandal was solved under Mrs Thatcher in 1984, the federalist drive began in earnest. The Single European Act signed in 1986 contained an element of supranational control in areas concerned with the single market, but, their appetite whetted for more power, federalists soon tabled proposals for Economic, Monetary and Political Union, representing momentous and radically new transfers of power to the centre.

It is essential to look beneath the political engineering in the proposed union treaties to assess how the tensions in Europe over past generations might be improved or worsened by the attempts to compress the many different countries and their separate interests into a legal structure, and whether this would be more or less likely to bring peoples together. Each country in the European Community has its own national interest to serve and undoubtedly does so. The problem with the pressure for federalism in the European Community is that so much of it is based on a lack of reality and of practical recognition of diverse national interests. Federalists claim that differences in culture, language and regard for law can be subsumed within their system, but in fact the forcing of different countries into their straitjacket will only exacerbate tensions. In their political immaturity, they believe that new constitutional arrangements can just be drawn up and engineered into the Community, forgetting that it is political freedoms, impulses and procedures which determine the kind of democratic decision-making upon which so many other matters depend, including freedom of choice, freedom of expression, freedom of speech and freedom of trade. Where these are genuinely available, voters can decide their priorities in their elections and national parliaments. This is democracy.

The United States has an interest in avoiding federalism in Europe. There has been much American pressure for greater integration in the past, but this is based on a certain lack of information about European politics and history, which are profoundly different from American. It is sometimes thought that the pressure exerted by the United States for greater European integration represents a reluctance by the United States to maintain its full commitment to and relationship with Britain. If such a policy was ever made explicit, it would be profoundly mistaken and would represent a failure by the United States to pursue its own self-interest in democracy, freedom of choice and freedom of trade, which are based on shared values and a common heritage and language. There would be little value to the United States in having Britain as its best friend in Europe if the purse-strings of the country were being pulled in Brussels or Frankfurt. As Winston Churchill said, the supreme fact about the twentieth century has been that the United States and the United Kingdom have marched together. This does not mean that Britain and the USA should exclude themselves from Europe, rather that they have a distinctive contribution to make.

The global economic village which we now inhabit demands that we maintain different centres of gravity within an interdependent world with no one fixed point where one country or continent can impose its will upon the others. Indeed, it is a clash of economic or political Titans which would create chaos. The notion of the European Community as a separate entity, creating Euro-champion companies and competing with the United States, Japan and other continental rivals is the very way to create the tension we need to avoid, particularly if it develops in a protectionist direction. Obsolete thinking, relevant only to the

1950s, should give way to a more flexible approach and take into account the disintegration of the system in Eastern Europe which denied democratic choice. Just as the world is becoming more multilateral and interdependent, and there are greater opportunities for mutual development and enterprise on a massive free-trade basis through the GATT, so it is less appropriate to break up the world into giant blocs of potential economic confrontation. This would be followed by hostility on a scale that has never been seen before.

The European federalists will make no contribution to political stability by neutering democracy and accountability. They are perhaps unaware of the dangers, since there is no level playing field in the constitutions of the European Community. Majority voting in the Council of Ministers would mean decision-making by government leaders sitting in camera, some of whom are simply not accountable to their Members of Parliament or to their electorates in the same way as British ministers. Some operate by decree, others without strongly rooted democratic traditions. Price stability is not something to be bought with the abandonment of democracy. The consequences of massive political decisions being taken on such a scale by majority voting would have profound implications, not only for Britain and for Europe, but also for the whole world.

It is essential to avoid the mistakes that were made after 1918 when political reform gave way to authoritarian bureaucratic notions of order and, in turn, to totalitarian repression. It would be most unwise of us to forget that this could happen again. Those in Eastern Europe have a clearer memory of what it was like and they warn us against its recurrence, as the author heard at a recent meeting in Prague.

It is the democratic tradition at Westminster which enabled us to engage in war in the Falklands and the Gulf. The nature of British democracy and political will enables us to understand when action has to be taken, however difficult it may seem to be. This marks out a particular difference between Britain and the rest of the European Community, with some exceptions, but it is a factor which cannot be avoided or ignored. A failure of political will when it is most needed or an acquiescence in autocratic methods of government are two sides of the same coin. Britain wants to co-operate fully with Germany and the other member states as a member of the European Community, but not on terms which would destroy her independence. When we speak of joining a political union, we must understand that it would be impossible for us to avoid the loss of our traditional strengths by so doing. The British approach is sometimes said to be a pragmatic one, but where democracy and the survival of parliamentary government are concerned, our stand must be one of principle.

2

Free Trade in the Global Village?

> Rather than treating the foreign investor as a rival, we should consider him a valuable helper, for he increases our production and the efficiencies of our business.
>
> Alexander Hamilton, 1791.

When the founding treaties of the Community were signed in the 1950s, emphasis was laid on the necessity for competition and free market forces, especially in the Treaty of Rome. It seemed that lessons had been learned from the protectionism of the inter-war period. Since then, the most significant reform in the EC's history was the signing of the Single European Act in 1986. The initial drive for a single European market came largely from the Thatcher government following a major policy speech at Chatham House in March 1984 by Sir Geoffrey Howe, the then Foreign Secretary. The Government had two objectives: first to improve the country's relations with the Community, damaged by years of squabbling over the Community's demonstrably unfair agricultural and budgetary mechanisms, which had severely disadvantaged Britain, and, second, to fulfil what was understood to be the explicit goal of the Treaty of Rome, the establishment of a free trade zone based upon economic co-operation between member states. This involved the abolition of barriers to the free movement of persons, goods, services and capital; all of which accorded well with prevailing Conservative liberal economics with the emphasis on free trade and consumer choice. The language was that of co-operation, not compulsion.

Now, however, the Treaty of Rome, which Mrs Thatcher once called a 'charter of economic liberty', is in danger of being transformed into one of central economic and political planning. This has political implications for democracy and accountable government within the EC, but also for the stability of world trade, since the Community's dirigiste thinking threatens to prevent agreement on liberalising trade in the GATT talks.

Britain and the EC have much to lose from protectionist measures. Within the EC certain countries, like France and Italy, who are riddled with protectionist instincts, have always been extremely sceptical about free trade and the importance of GATT. For example, at the end of July 1991 the French foreign trade minister, Dominique Strauss-Kahn, warned that on no account would France surrender its agricultural and industrial policies in the Uruguay Round. Volkswagen, which is the largest European car producer, has in recent months aligned itself behind the car protectionist lobby because, heavily dependent on high cost German labour, it is aware that it will have difficulties in beating off Japanese cars when they are imported without quotas into Europe. Perhaps the clearest example of dirigiste philosophy is the notion of national or European 'champion' companies.

The notion of champions is based on the false belief that protection from competition leads to long-term strength, but, as one economist has shown, where rivals cluster they are forced to innovate and compete most.[1] The supreme example of where national champions reign is Italy, where four mega-conglomerates dominate the economy. Yet it is noticeable that Italy's most successful industries are those which are subjected to the greatest degree of competition domestically, such as the tile and ceramic producers, or the clothing business. In Britain interventionist policies in the car industry produced British Leyland. BL came to rely on large cash hand-outs and subsidies, and eventually had to be cut down into its constituent elements and returned to the private sector. In Japan, by contrast, no single car-producer dominates, and the impetus for ever greater innovation and lower prices springs less from international competition than from the intense rivalry within Japan itself. Economic dirigisme merely legitimates the use of political power to protect powerful vested interets: the Italian economy and political class are largely in thrall to the big companies.

Protectionism is also rife in such areas as the electronics and semiconductor industries. The electronics industry will have received a total of 5.7 billion ecus from Brussels between 1990 and 1994, with additional money from national coffers. Europe's semi-conductor producers, mainly France and Holland, are campaigning to maintain the present 40% level of tariffs on imports. It is impossible to see why such protectionism will make the key players, Philips, SGS-Thomson and Siemens, more competitive against the Japanese firms, NEC and Toshiba, or the American Intel and Motorola. As the British have argued: 'Tariffs push up the price of computers, which use semiconductors, dampening the worldwide competitiveness of Europe's computer industry'.[2] The Japanese, who are the EC's main supplier of semi-conductors anyway, and a major player in computers, win despite the tariffs. Europe is the loser.

The Socialist French Prime Minister, Edith Cresson, whose government is supported in office by one of the few unreformed Communist parties in Europe, is known for her comments about 'little yellow men' from Japan. This typifies the attitude to Japan and Japanese investment in France and in the Community. (Mme Cresson's Minister for Employment is Jacques Delors's daughter.) It is as myopic as it is offensive. There seems little readiness in Europe to learn from the Japanese. On being taken over by Fujitsu, ICL was expelled from the European Computer Trade Group and forced to leave three EC collaborative projects, yet for some reason, IBM was allowed to participate. The gains to be had from Japanese investment and trade are comparable to those that American companies such as Ford and General Motors brought to Europe generations ago. They soon became real multi-nationals, as will Japanese companies.[3] We in Britain gained much from accepting United States investment. Today the UK owns £80 billion worth of investments in the US. The world has become so inter-dependent that we now see IBM Japan exporting American computers built in Japan to the EC. Japan has invested phenomenal sums in the Community. Between March 1987 and March 1990 direct investment in the EC grew from $6.5 billion to $42 billion. Britain received approximately half this. Its effect has been dramatic, especially in transforming the British manufacturing sector. For the first time since the 1950s the UK is now a net exporter of television sets. By the late 1990s we could also become a net exporter of cars because of heavy investment by Nissan, Honda and Toyota. As *The Economist* put it in a wide ranging analysis: 'European business needs more competition, not less'.[4]

This alone suggests that there is a serious danger of the European Community becoming based on an absurd paradox: that of internal free trade but external protectionism. It is a paradox that can only damage the Community's own long-term interests, and those of countries which the Community currently professes to wish to help, notably Eastern Europe and the old USSR. It is extraordinary that it is easier for the EC to export to Hungary, Czechoslovakia and Poland than it is for those countries to export to the EC. This is 'the reverse of the normal trading relationship between relatively strong and relatively weak economies'.[5] If the new democracies are denied markets for their goods, then they will be unable to obtain the hard currency they urgently need in order to carry out the far-reaching reforms that will modernise their economies. France prevented the EC from importing Polish beef in September 1991 and this attitude is all of a piece with their burning of British lamb.[6] A leading Czech politician has said, 'Why should Czechoslovakia be sacrificed on the altar of the Bavarian farmer?'[7] It is the fear of exclusion rather than the positive desire to be included that is driving these countries to apply for EC membership. In the wider Europe there is no enthusiasm for a political federation of EC states. The effects of EC protectionism in agriculture will continue to be gravely detrimental to other developing nations, especially in starving Africa.

But even internally within the EC, protectionism is highly damaging, both economically and politically, for the notion of sponsoring either national or EC-wide champions distorts fair competition and the level playing field. The 1992 programme has begun to falter amid growing evidence that it has become rigged with national interests, disadvantaging those countries who play by the rules.

The easiest way some choose to opt out of the obligations under the Single European Act is to ignore the Single Market directives. Implementation of directives has been hopelessly inadequate in some countries, notably Greece and Italy. Monitoring of such implementation and enforcement has been and remains insufficient. It is astonishing, given the need for monitoring, that the Commission's Sixth Report on the Completion of the Internal Market, published in June 1991, makes almost no reference at all to the enforcement of provisions of the single market, and although there is an account showing which national parliaments have legislated on the directives, implementation at national level is only one side of the coin: the report does not address implementation at local level. If directives are not being enforced at a local level, the EC market will remain unfair.

The most important instrument of dirigisme is subsidy, even though subsidy in a free market in a contradiction in terms. Article 92 of the Treaty of Rome forbids 'any aid granted by a member state which distorts or threatens to distort competition'. Yet the scale of subsidy in the European Community is staggering: although marginally declining, it represented an average 89 billion ecu a year from 1981 to 1986, and 82 billion ecu from 1986 to 1988. Agriculture takes 11 billion ecu a year of this, coal 13 billion ecu and railways 36 billion ecu, with the balance going to industry. Italy is by far the worst offender. In spite of a budget deficit which the government seems unable to control, Italy spends 9.6 billion ecu a year on industrial aid, which represents an average subsidy per employee of 3,136 ecu. Greece has an even higher per capita figure, 3,545 ecu. Approximately fifteen subsidy investigations have recently been underway in the European Commission. These include the French subsidy of 6 billion francs for Groupe Bull, the 287 billion lire for the reconstruction of the Italian trucking industry and 35 billion Belgian francs for a plan to recapitalise the state-owned airline, Sabena.

Another matter of concern with regard to the single market is the availability in some countries of unfair and uncompetitive cheap loans. Given the culture in some countries, such as Germany, where banks readily give subsidised loans to industries in which they have a stake, it seems impossible to put an end to them. In the author's constituency, for example, there is a company whose main competitor in Germany has been given switchgear free of charge by the local electricity board, and they have been given a twenty-year loan at no interest for generating plant.[8] As the brochure for the Kreditanstalt für Wiederaufbau (Credit Institute for Reconstruction) indicates in relation to Europe 1992:

> For a long time KFW has been promoting in particular the small and medium scale sector of the economy, i.e. it grants loans at favourable interest rates to small and medium sized enterprises to make up for their specific financing disadvantages...By extending its financing programmes, KFW aims at facilitating cross-border investments and joint ventures. *The offer is addressed to German companies investing in EC partner companies and foreign companies investing in the Federal Republic of Germany.* Funds on particularly favourable terms are available for investment projects that serve environmental protection in the Federal Republic of Germany and in regions bordering on the Federal Republic. Loans for environmental protection are offered at 0.5% lower than other loans, which are currently running at 8%.

It is very difficult to see how this approach can be reconciled to either Article 92 of the Rome Treaty or to the notion of fair competition in a single market.

Steel-casting companies in Spain which in Britain would have been bankrupted are continuing to offer steel-castings at artificially low prices, and indeed inefficient capacity and production is not only being maintained but is even being purposely created; while in France the producers of steel-castings are benefiting from soft loans from mostly state-owned banks.[9] It clear that it is costing British jobs on a substantial scale and that it will continue until the unfair practices cease. This may be a pious hope. Banking policy, both in Germany and in France, is far more geared to industry than is the case in the United Kingdom and there is considerable pressure on the German government to maintain grossly inefficient production in East Germany, which it can do by enlisting the aid of the banks.

If the single market is to come about, it will require far more impartiality within the European Commission. Although the Commissioners are committed not to be swayed by the national interests of their own countries, it is clear that Sir Leon Brittan, the Competition

Commissioner, has come up against stiff opposition from his colleagues when he has investigated anti-competitive behaviour in some of their countries, most recently over his veto of the Franco-Italian takeover of De Havilland in October 1991. Jacques Delors's celebrated outburst over the fine levied against Renault was a case in point. Brittan was also opposed by the Dutch Commissioner, Frans Andriessen, when investigations were launched into the merger of two Dutch coffee companies, Douwe Egberts and Van Nelle in 1988, which gave them a 70% market share of the Benelux countries. With the support of the Belgian Commissioner, Karel Van Niert, Brittan was forced to climb down and accept the merger.

The other big obstacle to the fair development of the single market is the existence of barriers to trade and investment in other countries. Britain fares particularly badly out of this, because of her unusually open economy, since it is possible for continental rivals to make bids in Britain. Smaller firms in the UK are more vulnerable to takeovers because of the existence of a sophisticated Stock Exchange which encourages small companies to raise finance by being floated on the unlisted markets. There is also in the UK much more public information on company accounts and results than in countries like Italy, Spain, Portugal and Greece. In Germany, most companies are partnerships, rather than quoted companies, and they are exempt from disclosing information which could be of use to competitors. Before unfication, small to medium-sized firms employing generally less than 500 workers accounted for half the Federal Republic's GDP and employed two thirds of its workforce. Around 370,000 GmbHs (limited liability companies) exist and they are required to make nearly nothing public. Their accounts are primarily the taxman's and the banks' business. There are only 2,000 Aktiengesellchaften (public limited companies) in Germany which are subject to fairly tight disclosure rules as in the UK. But even many of these firms are immune from takeover, despite being publicly quoted, because a majority of the voting shares are held either by families or by institutions closely linked to the existing management. In Spain shareholdings are not disclosed and structural barriers are a serious inhibition for contested bids. In France, where shareholdings are not generally disclosed, seven of the ten companies are state owned and over half of the two hundred largest companies are family controlled. Even after the Chirac privatisation, France's state sector today represents 12% of the economy, a figure only exceeded by Italy, Greece and Portugal. Although some subsidiaries of state firms have been publicly floated, as in the case of Pechiney, the aluminium and packaging group, they remain immune from takeovers because of the government's significant shareholdings. In the Netherlands, many quoted companies have widespread share ownership but the shareholders are given little power and technical barriers to takeovers are very important. In Italy, out of over two hundred listed companies, only seven have 50% of their shares in public hands and five are understood to be effectively controlled by family groupings.

In Germany and the Netherlands, there are very important technical barriers, the main ones being the two-tier board structure. In Germany this delays changes in the management boards and often on the supervisory board. In the Netherlands change in either board is practically impossible. In Germany other barriers include the issuing of non-voting shares, shares with restricting voting rights, poor access to share registers (where they exist) and the power of the three principal banks, who act as depositories, shareholders and as members of the supervisory boards. For example, the Allianz group in Munich has close to 25% of the Bavarian Hypo Bank, one of Germany's biggest. Mr Klaus Gotte, former finance chief of Allianz and now boss of a Munich-based engineering group, MAN, is supervisory board chairman of the Hypo. Allianz has 25% of Münchener Rückversicherung (Munich Re), the world's biggest reinsurance group, which in turn has 25% of Allianz. Both Munich Re and Allianz have stakes in a holding company which has more than 25% of MAN.

These obstacles have made it very difficult for British companies to launch takeovers on the continent, despite the fact that in 1988 the aggregate value of foreign takeovers in the UK amounted to around £35 billion, which was 73% by value of the EC total, followed by France with a mere 10% of the takeovers; in 1990 over £30 billion worth of UK firms fell into foreign ownership, that is over four times the comparable figure in France, Germany or Spain. On the other hand, UK firms only acquired a mere £4.2 billion of European assets in 1990, which was less than the French and even the Swedes.[10] As the House of Commons Foreign Affairs Committee reported:

> However strong the commitment of the UK's EC partners to the Single Market may be, extensive cultural and institutional barriers to the operation of free markets and to full industrial competition will remain. They stand in sharp contrast to the more open, and accessible, British model.[11]

This is particularly galling in areas where Britain is strong. British insurance companies have found the German market closed to them. Britain welcomes foreign investment, as everybody knows, but the point of having a European Community is to make everyone play by the rules. In the EC the rules are not being observed.

The French approach to takeovers has tended to aim at strengthening their central manufacturing core and to ensure that the French company remains dominant and in control, whereas the British takeover is generally aimed at diversification. Frequently the French company seeks to take over second tier United States enterprises already established in Europe with a view to establishing itself as a mainstream European producer. An example of this was the takeover by CGE through a subsidiary, Alcatel, of the European telecommunications side of ITT in 1986. It thereby created the largest telecommunications company in Europe at the time. Another case is that of Bull, the French nationalised computer manufacturer, which acquired a 65% controlling interest in the American company, Honeywell, and then in 1989 of the microcomputer company, Zenith, to become one of the largest computer companies in Europe.

Similar takeovers have been launched by the French chemical company, Rhone-Poulenc (which recently spent over £3 billion in acquisitions), by Usinor-Sacilor and by Renault. All three companies have been in receipt of money raised by 'unusual' means. Rhone-Poulenc pioneered a technique for raising cash by issuing exotic securities which have the quality of both debt and equity.

Usinor-Sacilor received £250 million in July 1991 from the state-owned bank, Credit Lyonnais. This, like the illegal subsidies Renault received, is now being investigated by the Commission. It would appear that much of France's corporate aggrandisement has been undertaken by state-owned companies, many of which have been in receipt of illicit subsidies. Under Britain's liberal regime vast acquisitions have been made in the UK by Credit Lyonnais, the Elf Aquitaine state-controlled oil group and Thomson CSF in defence electronics. The British Monopolies and Mergers Commission did review these bids but dismissed fears that the deals were tantamount to backdoor nationalisation.

In Germany there is a strong defensive intra-German strategy to prevent the taking over of German companies by foreigners. This was well illustrated by the refusal of the authorities in Germany to allow GEC to purchase the then nearly bankrupt electrical company AEG following objections from the German trade unions. AEG was subsequently purchased by Daimler Benz.

Strategically driven transactions are noticeable in Germany. The big AGs (PLCs) have plenty of 'hidden reserves' because they are obliged to only reveal 'partial' operating profits publicly, so there is in fact much more money stashed away for takeovers than a glimpse at corporate balance sheets would suggest.

Towering over the Mittelstand (medium-sized) companies are vast national champions like Daimler-Benz, Siemens, Bertelsmann, Deutsche Bank and Allianz. With the launch of the single market programme, all have gone on massive spending sprees. These could become European champions, most notably Volkswagen, which recently purchased Seat in Spain, Skoda in Czechoslovakia and has built a factory in East Germany. VW is keen to obtain the benefits of cheap labour. At the same time this has been accompanied by a determined push by the German authorities through the EC institutions to impose a Community-wide statutory minimum wage to counter the high wage costs of West Germany.

The fear is that the current trend of mergers and joint ventures within the Community, far from promoting competition, may in fact stifle it, as has been the case with Bull in France, for example. In 1986/87, 70% of mergers involved firms with combined sales of over 1 billion ecus, whereas the figure in 1988/89 was over 90%. This suggests that national and EC monoliths are developing with the connivance of both national and EC authorities.

Taken together, these structures are stringently protectionist. They make it very difficult for British firms to make acquisitions, especially hostile bids, and show the 'single market' to be in reality a very one-sided affair, pivoted far too much against British interests. Now moves are afoot to mend the situation. The real problem, however, is that it is a race against time. A number of amendments have been introduced into EC Company Law directives currently under consideration. But as one commentator has remarked, 'the trouble is some of these directives look as if they may take until the 21st century to be adopted, let alone implemented'.[12] If implemented, the Fourth Directive would force annual accounts to be made more public and the crucial Fifth Directive would end the abuse of special voting rights and outlaw existing or potential technical barriers. It does, however, propose a two-tier board enabling employee participation, something the British strongly oppose. It currently appears unlikely that either directive will be implemented before the end of 1991 because of disputes over the whole Company Law Statute, which the Germans in particular are not happy about. The Institute of Directors has pointed out that 'the 5th Company Law Directive has been under discussion since 1972, with no agreement yet in sight'.[13] The 13th Company Law Directive will put an end to the more blatant 'poison pill' tactics that enable companies under threat of takeover to make themselves unappetising. The directive would also lay down minimum requirements for the conduct of takeovers, effectively superseding the City of London's Takeover Panel. It would, unfortunately, put an end to informal advice in takeovers which prevents unnecessary litigation. Rules laid down in a statute would be less flexible.

In the meantime, however, until these directives are enforced, Britain's corporate landscape will remain open to attack without a right to reply in kind.

The setting of EC standards is an example of where national interests are quickly interwoven into the fabric of the single market ideal. Until very recently it was conspicuous that the secretariats and standards committees were dominated by Germans who fought to have German standards, which are often the strictest in the world, adopted as definitive EC standards. British industrialists took time to appreciate what was happening. However, the task of setting EC wide standards remains daunting and progress has been slow. According to the Commission's Standards Office, another 1,000 EC standards will be needed by 1992 if the single market is to come about. In 1990 the CEN and CENELEC institutes, the two main European standard making bodies, published only 293 EC standards. The cost of implementing EC standards is proving to be very serious for Britain's small and medium sized firms. The Institute of Directors warns that the European Commission has overlooked the distortion to competition which is arising between smaller and larger companies as a result of the moves to set EC-wide standards.[14] For smaller companies, especially those engaged in craft industries, the combined cost of monitoring equipment, inspection and certification is proving so high as to threaten their existence. This could undermine the enterprise economy and lead to a reduction in consumer choice. The report stresses that the entire standardisation process could be devalued by inspectors concentrating on minor infractions of the rules and on monitoring products manufactured outside their own country. This could distort competition and reduce support in the business community for the single market.

The opening up of public procurement to competition beyond national borders is a good example of what the single market is all about. The most competitive firms providing the best service at the lowest price are the ones which should prosper. However, the degree to which this is actually happening is minimal. Only 2% of major public sector contracts are going across EC frontiers. In spite of directives ensuring compliance and enabling the Commission to take offenders to the Court of Justice, the situation is little changed. The requirement that purchasers accept 'the most economically advantageous bid' seems invariably to be favouring national bidders. It is disconcerting that businessmen believe procurement will remain a national affair. Yet, for a company like Siemens in Germany which relies on public contracts for a third of its sales, it is hard to see how German politicians are going to risk alienating the electorate and create unemployment by placing lucrative public contracts outside the Federal Republic. The situation clearly needs to be monitored, but it is extremely difficult to prove discrimination and few bidders would wish to alienate potential clients. Anecdotal evidence suggests that British companies, which in theory stand a good chance of winning public contracts, are finding in practice that they are being discouraged. For example, in one case a number of Staffordshire businessmen were keen to make a bid for a £75 million contract for the construction of security fencing around a British military base in Germany. The Property Services Agency told the businessmen that it was hardly worth their while because there was no doubt that the German government had every intention of awarding the contract to a German company.

Much of this is having a deleterious effect on British industry and jobs. It is often said that Britain's membership of the Community is good for British business, and attention is drawn to the volume of our trade with the Community. In fact, our trade with the EC is overwhelmingly in deficit. Between 1970 and 1989 the UK had an accumulated trade deficit with the rest of the EC of £86.4 billion in current prices, whereas our accumulated trade surplus with the rest of the world was £78.8 billion in the same period. The situation has worsened since our membership of the Community. In 1970 before we joined the Common Market our trade with Europe yielded a surplus of £1.9 billion. The deficit is now particularly high with Germany: in 1990 it was £6.7 billion, that is three times higher than with any other country. The general trend in the last four years is towards a growing deficit. Between 1986 and 1990 the UK deficit with Germany rose by over £1 billion, although this has temporarily improved.

It is unclear with the development of the single market whether statistics will continue to be maintained on a national basis or whether these will be subsumed into a blancmange of European statistics. Any move in this direction should be resisted because it is vital as part of the monitoring process to see what impact the single market is having on our national economy.

In addition to the adverse economic effect, the trend in which the single market programme is moving will have a serious political effect as well. It is clear from the above that the rules are being bent to the benefit of some. This is occurring at the same time as the Commission is using the single market as an excuse to augment its power for political means. The Frankfurt Institute has warned that the quest for an internal market has rapidly become a pretext for unrelated transfers of power and international standardisation by decree. Federalists have resorted to 'unnecessary centralisation and bureaucratic harmonisation in the European Community'.[15] This has been demonstrated by the abuse of the SEA's provisions for majority voting and harmonisation under Article 100A. For example, this free trade article has been wrongly used to draw up radical measures banning tobacco advertising, a matter which has nothing to do with free trade, and a pure case of Commission empire-building. This is rightly causing deep concern in the British newspaper and advertising industries. It has serious implications for the freedom of the press, as shown at a European Conference in Luxembourg on 3 July 1991.

Nor do these impulses come simply from the Commission itself. Nobody will deny that the Commission has an overwhelmingly Franco-German flavour, and this is already reflected in its economic priorities. The danger is clear: that the Commission will increase its power to interfere in national economies in the name of 'Europe' while in fact serving national interests of one or other country.

The Social Charter, for instance, has nothing to do with the single market. There is no earthly reason why the Community should have harmonised social benefits. (Do the British want the National Health Service abolished by European directive?) It is notable that the one country which stands to lose most by free competition in labour is Germany, where labour and social costs are highest. The Social Charter will impose similar wages on the otherwise low-wage economies of the EC, reducing their competitiveness and safeguarding jobs in Germany. Moreover, with its restrictions on night work and part-time work and its minimum wage policy, it is a throwback to the damaging socialist policies of the 1970s, and will only cause unemployment. (Germany's unemployment has for long been extremely high, and is currently catastrophically so in the former East Germany.)

Another example is merger policy. The Commission is currently demanding greater powers to pronounce on merger policy over the heads of the member states. In March 1991 it won an important case when the strongly integrationist European Court of Justice condoned Brussels' ability to rule on public service monopolies without the approval of EC member states, despite the fact that the Court's principal legal adviser, the Advocate General, called for the Commission's powers to be restricted under Article 90 of the Treaty of Rome. The British Minister for Corporate Affairs, John Redwood, is worried that these powers will be misused for purposes other than competition, such as regional policy or national champions.[16] It will augment the Commission's power to tinker around with the European economy for its own purposes, or in the interest of its more powerful members.

One of the driving forces behind some supporters of a single European market is the desire to create a European superstate. This political objective is perceived as needing pan-European companies capable of overwhelming international competition. The Commission has elected to promote European 'champions' which will dominate the EC market, in the hope that they will be able to outperform international giants in the United States and Japan. It is not difficult to guess which countries will benefit from this supranational politico-economic Lego. The 19th-century German economist Friedrich List argued for just such a policy to build the emerging German empire: in the same way, the manipulation of the economy would be used for political nation-building, and it would inevitably be controlled by the most powerful country, if not deliberately, then by default. Just as the 21st century requires a more diffused and safer balance of interest in what needs to be an increasingly multilateral global village, there is a risk of economic, institutional and political power being centralised in the European Community, and that a new bout of economic empire-building may occur. The Euro institutionalists see Japan and the United States as if they were multi-national companies rather than countries, and they seem to be trying to respond in kind, as if they were the directors of Europe Ltd. It is true that one of the features of Japan and Germany is the intimate nexus between industry and political power, which gives some credence to this view. But companies are not democratic institutions and the nations of Europe are not companies. Economics must not come before democratic politics. A failure to understand this essential point could lead to more than a trade war.

The sheer recklessness and shortsightedness of the Commission, and especially the Franco-German axis within it, is nowhere clearer than in the GATT fiasco. The current Uruguay Round of GATT talks aims to liberalise trade in agriculture, textiles and financial services. Upon these negotiations hinges the future of international trade. If they are not successfully concluded in the next few months a major objective of the single market will not have been achieved: far from becoming more internationally efficient and competitive, EC industry will fall further behind in a world of growing protectionism and trade blocs.

In recent years the two guiding principles of non-discrimination and multilateralism which have lain at the heart of the GATT system have been gradually eroded. Increasingly GATT rules have been breached either in spirit or rule by states, not least in the EC, by resorting to protectionist measures such as quotas on textiles or Voluntary Restraint Agreements on Japanese car imports. Increased discrimination has occurred with the flowering of preferential trading arrangements like those with former European colonies and the EC, enshrined in the Lomé Agreement. Worst of all, agricultural protectionism has grown to such absurd proportions, particularly in the EC, that there is no free market in agricultural produce. The EC and the USA both dump their subsidised food on world markets at artificially low prices which robs developing countries of any outlet for their own surplus foodstuffs, as they cannot compete against the industrial world's $126 billion of annual subsidies.

The point has now been reached where radical action is called for in order to salvage GATT. The Americans have demanded a reduction of 75% in subsidies to agriculture across the board. The EC has offered 30%. The talks have been extended beyond their December 1990 deadline by one year. If the EC fails to budge further on agricultural reform, then GATT will fail. The trouble is that the French and German governments, swayed by their domestic farming electorates, have been unwilling to accept radical reform of CAP, even if it means access to foreign markets in which the EC is better able to compete.

If the GATT talks fail, those EC industries which are already internationally competitive and world leaders will be penalised the most. EC industries like financial services and telecommunications which have most to gain from global deregulation and liberalisation of trade will find themselves excluded from foreign markets because of the EC's protectionism being reciprocated in East Asia, Japan and the United States. Yet the gains from liberalising trade in services alone are worth $600 billion a year. The EC would benefit greatly from this. The Commission should not be swayed by the siren voices of the protectionist coalition of farmers and EC giants like Daimler-Benz, Philips and Olivetti. The future for the advanced industrial countries lies increasingly in a proper balance between manufacturing and the service sector. Even Japan, the most efficient manufacturing power, has started to farm out its production centres to low wage countries. In the US the most advanced clothes shops have computerised cash registers which monitor what garments have been sold on a given day. The list is sent off to workshops that night in Southeast Asia and replacements are in the stores within four days. This is the market economy par excellence. Britain's Marks and Spencer would thrive on such competition. Yet the EC's inward-looking reaction is to block the winds of competition.

Unless the Common Agricultural Policy is radically reformed, the Uruguay Round will collapse. The CAP has reached such absurd proportions that it is now damaging everybody's interests – the producers, the consumers and the Third World. Unless it is quickly overhauled, there will be long lasting damage to trans-Atlantic relations, to the environment and to the competitiveness of EC industry. There is now a 30 million tonne 'world record' grain surplus, as Boris Johnson showed on 19 October 1991 in the *Spectator*.

The cost to the consumer in Britain amounts to £830 per family in higher food prices. The CAP will cost the EC £27.6 billion in subsidies and price support mechanisms in the next year. For an industry which, as Frans Andriessen, the External Affairs Commissioner, has pointed out, accounts for only 5% of EC exports compared to the 25% of the population in industrial work and the even larger percentage in financial services, agriculture is absurdly mollycoddled. The CAP was designed to help the EC's 14 million farmers: instead, it promotes inefficient farmers at the expense of the efficient UK farmer, destroys the international market to the detriment of the Third World and cheats EC taxpayers.

Moreover, the degree of fraud which it engenders is astounding. According to a study made in 1989 by Professor Klaus Tiedemann of Freiburg University, fraud accounts for an estimated 10% of the EC budget, or about £6 billion a year. This amounts to between £20 and £60 billion lost to fraud in the 1980s. Most of this fraud stems directly from CAP by way of its export subsidies, border taxes, price support mechanism and its subsidies for currency fluctuations.

Unfortunately, fraud in itself has not been a sufficient inducement to force agricultural reform. Mrs Thatcher fought to have it put at the top of the agenda at the EC Summit in June 1989. She was reprimanded by an indignant Jacques Delors who said that fraud is a 'phony controversy' and a 'distraction' from important matters, like the 'real' issue of economic and monetary union. Yet this 'distraction', which the Commission's own Court of Auditors Reports have warned, costs hundreds of millions of pounds, was dismissed as accounting for no more than 0.18% of farm spending. This was a figure plucked out of the air by the Commission who know that the scale of fraud is not adequately monitored. The readiness of EC officials to discount the whole issue is a cause for grave concern. The EC gets irritated at the mention of fraud because it fears that it weakens the Commission's hand in GATT talks. Yet CAP as a whole is threatening EC prosperity and global free trade.

In July 1991 the Agricultural Commissioner, Raymond MacSharry, produced the most radical plan for reform since the CAP was introduced nearly thirty years ago. That the MacSharry Plan for agricultural reform are the only proposals the Commission can produce hardly bodes well. The Plan will penalise the EC's efficient farmers, notably the British, to the benefit of the small ones, the French and Germans. It will do little to end the real problem, that of a heavily protected EC market in which surplus production is encouraged by vast subsidies, which amount to almost 60% of the EC budget. 'Some people say no reform would be better than one which destroys the agriculture of the most efficient, provides an open cheque that must increase costs year in, year out, pensions the part-timer and leaves the consumer and taxpayer to bear the burden'.[17]

If the GATT talks break down, the consequences could be dire. A recent study by the Centre for International Economics in Canberra suggests that it would cost the EC $52 billion a year. If the Community's protectionism was met by US retaliation, the EC would lose $132 billion and the US $64 billion a year, while proving particularly damaging to the economies of Eastern Europe. Arthur Dunkel, the Director-General of GATT, has warned that the impact would be 'catastrophic', with Europe losing tens of thousands of jobs.

A successful outcome would be enormously beneficial. Between 1946 and 1985 the volume of world trade grew nine times; it increased at twice the rate of output and incomes. It is estimated that agreement on the whole GATT package could increase global economic activity by $4,000 billion within a decade.[18] The US trade representative has said it would be like writing a cheque for $17,000 payable over ten years for every family of four in the world.[19]

The situation will be made more dangerous if the EC cuts itself off from the new North American Free Trade Area.[20] It is notable that the US Congress has recently granted President Bush fast-track authority to negotiate both the Uruguay Round and the North American Free Trade Area, showing the importance they attach to a favourable outcome in both.

They realise that a free-trade solution is required:

> the key to success will depend as much on political courage as diplomatic skill. In a fast-moving, interdependent world, political courage is sometimes in both short supply and high demand...The key, however, will be to move toward a more market-oriented basis and not to look to the government for protection. This reality may be the most difficult one of all to accept.[21]

That the Community is now striving for political and monetary union reflects the successful hijacking of the SEA by the federalists. It may prove to be a Pyrrhic victory. For the internal market programme is by no means completed; on the contrary, much remains to be done. For Britain, the country with the most open market and one of the best records in implementing EC directives, the refusal by other member states to end these protectionist tendencies is very serious indeed. If the fruits of the single market are not going to be realised, then there can be precious little incentive to go along with political and economic union, even if we wanted to.

3

Sovereignty and EMU

> The fault, dear Brutus, is not in our stars
> But in ourselves, that we are underlings.
>
> Shakespeare, *Julius Caesar.*

The debate over the future development of the Community has been divided into two topics for the purposes of the Intergovernmental Conferences, Economic and Monetary Union, and Political Union. They are intimately connected, for as this chapter will show, acceptance of monetary union implies *de facto* acceptance of political union. They are the same thing.

The first argument to scotch is that Britain has committed itself over the years to accepting the single currency and the central bank. One phrase which is often adduced in support of this thesis is the phrase in the preamble to the Treaty of Rome, 'determined to lay the foundations of an ever closer union among the peoples of Europe'. This is taken to mean that the EC must become ever more integrated. Such an interpretation is false. Clearly the phrase can mean anything one likes: it would be difficult for anybody to refuse to sign up to such a worthy aim as international understanding. Yet on any interpretation, the 'peoples of Europe' can never be restricted to the peoples of the European Community, and therefore the 'ever closer union' has nothing to do with the EC itself. The sentiment expressed in the phrase is simply that a strong EC should lay these foundations for the whole continent. This has become more important since the changes in Eastern Europe and the USSR.

The second argument is that the governments of the EC have committed themselves to the goal of Monetary Union in communiqués at the end of summits in the past. It is true that a commitment was made to the 'progressive realisation of economic and monetary union' in 1972, but the meaning of the phrase was never defined at that stage.

The Single European Act (1986) does, however, define it: as 'Co-operation in Economic and Monetary Policy'. This is perfectly acceptable, indeed desirable. The relevant chapters speak of 'co-operation' in these fields (budgetary policy, exchange rate policy, etc.) and of the 'advisory' role of the Monetary Committee. Nowhere does it speak of central control. Thus, there are no commitments to accepting the plan for a central bank.[1]

No doubt many in the EC have long wished to see a Delors Report version of monetary union imposed in order to further their federalist aims. Like many other things in the Community, however, the impetus came more from the internal tensions within the Community, and from the self-interest of its members than from loftier aims. In particular, the desire for EMU comes largely from Italian and French resentment at the dominant position of the Bundesbank within the European Monetary System.

In theory, the EMS is a means by which the currencies of the EC are maintained at a stable exchange rate with one another; in practice, it means all the weaker currencies aligning themselves to the strongest, the Deutsche Mark. The Germans have frequently allowed the Deutsche Mark to rise beyond its permitted range, leaving the central banks of the weaker currencies to intervene to support them. This has placed the burden of keeping the Mark systematically undervalued on the central banks of the poorer countries, who often have to resort to borrowing to finance their currency-support interventions. This helps keep Germany's huge surplus of exports competitively priced. The Germans have taken the view that 'domestic price stability must have priority over exchange rate stability',[2] leaving it up to others to ensure the latter. They have been able to get away with it, because it is difficult to reproach the Germans for pursuing an excessively sound monetary policy and sticking to low inflation.[3]

The French have long chafed at the bit. In 1983 they even considered leaving the EMS; since then they have been obliged to keep their interest rates 2% or 3% higher than in Germany, in pursuit of a strong franc. The most noticeable effect of this has been very high levels of unemployment in France (2.8 million in October 1991). Germany, by contrast, with a huge export surplus, benefits from the systematic undervaluation of her currency in a way that net importers do not. Moreover,

> the French are convinced that the Germans want to preserve their monetary hegemony as EMU approaches: the more dominant the Mark is, the more Germany will be able to dictate conditions and draw up plans for a European central bank based on the Bundesbank. A senior French official... explains, 'What is disturbing in the German attitude is that it

> betrays a very hegemonial mentality. Germany wants all the European currencies at her feet, and she is on the point of abusing her dominant position.'[4]

The Italians joined the French by attacking the deflationary effect of Germany's dominant position on their economy.[5] They felt that this prevented other countries from ever catching up with her. These protests may have been ignored had it not been for the enthusiasm of Hans-Dietrich Genscher for EMU: 'the creation of a single European monetary zone, with a European central bank, constitutes the economically indispensable centrepiece of a European single market'.[6]

Ever since, the role of the Germans in determining the timing and nature of EMU has been dominant. Given that the main impetus behind EMU is the desire of the French to get a seat on the Bundesbank,[7] and given the fact that the Germans hold all the aces, this is hardly surprising. Formerly, the difference between the Germans and the French was that the Germans wanted to await greater economic convergence before implementing a monetary union, while the French thought that this goal should be achieved by economic dirigisme, including monetary union.[8] By 1988, however, the Germans had accepted the principle of EMU and worked within the debate to achieve their aims.

The Germans had long demanded that any putative European central bank must be 'independent' of government control. Even before the discussions during and after the Delors Report (April 1989), the French had largely accepted the German demand. The former Prime Minister, Michel Rocard, declared, 'I am certainly a European federalist. The European Central Bank is absolutely necessary and we shall concede that it has to be politically autonomous to reassure the Germans'.[9] The *Financial Times* described the French attitude thus: 'independence [of the central bank] is a regrettable but unavoidable price to be paid to the Germans and the taboos of the Bundesbank'.[10] Other commentators have been quite frank about their desire to see the Germans run the show. Samuel Brittan writes, 'Will British monetary policy be made in Frankfurt – and eventually perhaps in Berlin? I very much hope so'.[11]

These concessions were made even before the Delors committee met. During the discussions, it is clear that the Germans played a decisive role, insisting right at the end of the discussions (at the penultimate meeting in March 1989) on binding rules on national budget deficits. The independence of the bank and its constitutional commitment to price stability were also accepted.[12]

Despite this, the Germans continued to manoeuvre on the question of EMU after the report was published. Indeed, for a while, the British Treasury thought they had an ally in the Germans in opposing the

Delors Report.[13] In this they were mistaken, but the Franco-German axis was not harmonious either. One of the moments of greatest strain came during the meeting at Ashford Castle in Ireland (April 1990) when it appears that the Germans suggested that the Deutsche Mark should become the single currency. This was not stated explicitly in the reports, but Delors became very angry during the meeting, saying, 'This [German] hostility to the ecu is dangerous. For political reasons the ecu must be developed',[14] and the *Financial Times* wrote of 'Bonn's disparagement of the European Currency Unit as the putative single currency'.[15] Even though the idea was firmly rejected, Pöhl was able to declare a month later that 'the German concept regarding the principles of a common European central bank has been accepted by most European governments'.[16] He had, after all, made it very clear that the Germans would never give up the Deutsche Mark unless what they got in return was just as good.[17]

German influence continued to be dominant as the discussions continued. Aware of German determination to maintain control over the currency, the Commission gave Pöhl a decisive say in drawing up the draft statutes of the proposed European Central Bank. In June 1990, the Bundestag determined that the bank should be sited in Frankfurt.[18] When the draft statutes were submitted to the European Council, *The Economist*, in an article entitled 'Karl-Otto Bismarck'[19] wrote: 'Mr Pöhl's influence over the 46 pages of detailed rules is not hard to spot.' The Germans had shifted their position since the writing of the Delors Report: where they had previously wanted 'binding rules' for budget deficits, they now called for 'sanctions' to be available to the Community as a means of enforcing the bank's decisions on recalcitrant member states.[20] Despite all this, doubts continue to exist on Germany's real commitment to EMU. Having indirectly made Mrs Thatcher pay with her political life for refusing to sign up to their timetable of achieving EMU by 1992, they are now blowing cold on the issue, as they are faced with a ballooning budget deficit of their own, and no longer need French and Community political support for reunification.[21]

During this period, they also set about rubbishing the British proposals for competing currencies, and for the hard ecu. They evidently prefer strict discipline and central control to fair competition. Count Lambsdorff, the former Economics Minister, now Chairman of the centrist FDP,[22] delivered a particularly strong attack on John Major's hard ecu plan, calling it 'nonsense'.[23] In doing so, he was merely echoing the views of Dr Pöhl who, although proudly 'independent' of the Bonn government, conducted all the German government's negotiations over EMU throughout 1989 and 1990.[24] This complicity between the Bundesbank and the government in Bonn is helped by the fact that the

Vice-President of the Bundesbank, Hans Tietmeyer, is Chancellor Kohl's personal financial adviser.

At around the time of the publication of the draft statutes for the proposed European central bank (November 1990), the Germans started calling for a quick move to a two-speed EMU, with only Germany's immediate neighbours joining the ecu zone.[25] They also began to press harder for moves to political union, and an increasing transfer of policy-making to the European level, especially to the European Parliament. The link between German agreement to EMU and their demands on political union was made explicit, and became another condition for their agreement. It was described as the 'price' the Germans would demand for giving up the Deutsche Mark.[26] The reason for this is that Germany's huge trade surplus is overwhelmingly with the Community (approx. 70% of it was with the EC, although in late 1991, there has been a significant drop, albeit temporarily, in Germany's surplus). She must protect her markets, and thus any control lost at the national level must be reimposed at the European level. As Pöhl says, the basic premise for monetary union must be a common economic and financial policy.[27] Furthermore, afraid that competition from low-wage countries will undermine employment in Germany, they want to safeguard their position via the Social Charter and the minimum wage. The situation will doubtless continue to change, especially as the initial euphoria over German and European unification being two sides of the same coin (the slogan trotted out repeatedly in 1990) becomes increasingly ludicrous, as the cost of East Germany spirals.[28] (The original idea had been to synchronise German unification with the single market, implementing both in 1993. In reality, not only will they not go together, but also German unification will perhaps slow EMU down.[29]) The Governor of the Bank of England called for a slow-down on 22 October 1991.

Playing hard to get is a game which can go on for some considerable time, especially if one has as ardent a suitor as the French. German officials have repeatedly threatened to leave the EC integration process unless they can have it their way. The German EC Commissioner warned the EC not to 'back Bonn into a corner' in making it decide between East Germany and the Community, saying that, if pushed, Germany would abandon the latter.[30] Chancellor Kohl, meanwhile, adopted a rather bullying tone by saying that German and European unification, like the flowing of the Rhine, are unstoppable and will wash away those who try to prevent them. He also has said that the choice is between political union in the EC and domination by Germany. It is difficult to think of more threatening language than to say that political union must be accepted if countries wish to avoid being dominated.[31]

One German paper commented frankly: 'Kohl wants to force political union with the Deutsche Mark crowbar'.[32]

The tactic used by the Commission for passing the Single European Act was to present it to the member states as if it were the only thing on offer: either take this or leave the Community.[33] In particular, 'Britain was bounced into surrenders of sovereignty which she would never have accepted if they had been presented as abstract ideas'.[34] The same ambiguous approach is being employed to achieve EMU. Other members of the Community make it clear that Monetary Union is the very centrepiece of Political Union, a symbol and real lever of political integration and central control. The new President of the Bundesbank, Helmut Schlesinger, has written, 'it is essentially political factors which have pushed the German government to promote Economic and Monetary Union. EMU is considered to be an important contribution to political union'.[35] Yet the British advocates of EMU, such as Sir Leon Brittan, prefer to dwell on the supposed practical benefits, playing down the political implications. It is all rather reminiscent of the Emperor Maximilian's remark to the future Charles V, 'My son, you go and deceive the English, and I will go and deceive the French'.[36]

One of the more pathetic arguments in favour of EMU is that it will save transaction costs between currencies. One MEP has calculated that if you start with £100 in Britain and change this sum successively into each of the Community's eleven currencies, you would only have £50 by the final transaction.[37] Frankly, only an MEP who spends his life flying around the Community at the taxpayer's expense, would think of conducting such a fatuous experiment. Even the Commission, with all its enthusiasm for EMU, could only come up with a potential saving of between 0.1% and 0.5% of the Community's GDP, and even this did not take into account new costs of changing the ecu into other, non-EC currencies. Indeed, it is amazing that Sir Leon Brittan should still refer to these 'costs'[38] long after Pöhl has said quite clearly that they are irrelevant: 'the repeated reference to alleged huge savings in transaction costs for the currencies of a single currency area are not in the least convincing'.[39] As one authority remarks, 'Europe tricks its way forward. Idealistic visions of the Community are intoned by governments: they get nowhere, but with repetition start to warp governments' view of normality'.[40]

The other argument which the Commission advances is that EMU would be an economic bonanza. Those who remember that membership of the Common Market was to be a bonanza, and who have seen Britain's trade deficit with the Community rise inexorably, will rightly be sceptical of this idea.[41] So will any sensible person who realises that the strength of an economy and the standard of living depend on the ability to sell goods and services, and not on monetary tinkering. Undeterred, the Commission insist that 'EMU, like 1992, is a positive-sum game'.[42] Elsewhere, they are less sanguine, covering the chronic weakness of their arguments in the figleaf of officialese: 'There are fundamental reasons why an aggregate estimate of the impact of economic and monetary union is not feasible. This is because economic and monetary union will cause a very complex chain of reactions: the systemic changes will lead to policy changes, and both will condition behavioural changes in the economy, before arriving at the final impacts in terms of economic well-being'.[43] Price stability, difficult as it is to define, is a worthy objective but does not depend upon independence of the banking system in itself.

Helmut Schlesinger has attacked the Commission for over-estimating the economic benefits and for under-estimating the risks of EMU, especially where the need for massive transfers from rich countries to poor ones is concerned. This is a worry echoed by John Major, while Chancellor, who warned that EMU would lead to 'huge political demand for resource transfers on a very large scale indeed'.[44] This is presumably what the poorer countries expect to get. The Governor of the Bank of England, Mr Robin Leigh-Pemberton, has said, 'if the Community moved to full Monetary Union before economic convergence was considerably greater, long-term structural problems could be aggravated, and some areas quite severely disadvantaged. This could be politically as well as economically divisive'.[45] Finally, Dr Pöhl, who resigned after German Monetary Union, has said, 'The adjustment pressure (after the abandonment of the exchange rate as an instrument of adjustment) would fall entirely on other aggregates, particularly on employment, and ever increasing public transfer payments would become inescapable. The German monetary union provides a spectacular lesson in this respect'.[46] Why do the Commission claim that it 'would have a positive impact on employment and on the balanced development of the regions'[47] when everyone else is aware of the dangers? The reason must surely be that, 'like most vigorous debates over economic policy, it is at least as much about power as about economics'.[48]

The fact is that there is no such thing as an 'independent' central bank. Some have accepted the Commission's argument (as it is presented in Britain) that monetary policy is something politically neutral. William Rees-Mogg has written, 'We need to have money which is a stable measure of value. If the Germans can provide this, we should be grateful to them just as the world ought to be grateful to us for having a zero line of longitude running constantly through Greenwich'.[49] It is difficult to think of a less appropriate analogy.

The Bundesbank is not independent: Article 12 of its constitution says, 'The Bundesbank is bound to support the general economic policy of the Federal Government.' This much should be clear after the Bundesbank under Pöhl was forced to accept Federal Government policy not only on the principle of German Monetary Union but also on the exchange rate, both of which it had initially resisted. Indeed, the Federal Government did not even consult the bank before making its announcement on GMU.[50] Membership of the ERM has necessitated a 'close co-operation between the Federal Government and the Bundesbank' since the government is responsible for exchange rate policy; and Pöhl and Schlesinger have both made it clear that they are obliged to obey their political masters on EMU as well.[51] The same is true of the Federal Reserve in the US: 'the Federal Reserve mechanism is not, in fact, independent *of the government* but it is independent *within the government*'.[52] In exactly the same way, the draft statutes for the proposed European Central Bank say, 'Without prejudice to the objective of price stability, the System shall support the general economic policy of the Community'.[53] The very fact that the supporters of federalism felt obliged to call a parallel conference on political union at the same time as the one of monetary union underlines that the two are inseparable.

It is not the constitution of the central bank which determines its success, it is the policies followed, and overall budgetary policies are as important as pure monetary policy. As the then Chancellor of the Exchequer, John Major, pointed out, 'an independent Fed in the US performed less well than a dependent central bank in Japan'.[54] Central bankers, like everyone else, live in the world: they are part of a society and decisions they take are political – but they are not elected. In some countries, at certain times, the consensus has been anti-inflationary: this has generally been the case in Germany, although the 'independent' Bundesbank has not prevented inflation being above 5% in eight of the last 20 years, quite apart from the monetary difficulties of German Monetary Union.[55] As Professor S.F. Bush said in *The Times* (7 October 1991), it was the commercial banks not the Bank of England which generated the credit explosion in 1987-89: 'A central bank, whether independent or not, is an almost total irrelevance as far as inflation is concerned in a world dominated by thousands of different monetary agencies switching assets and liabilities across the world at the touch of a button.' In the US during the 1970s, the cultural climate in economic thinking was soft on inflation, and the Fed did not tackle it as a result, even though it had the power to do so.[56] While in Germany 'there is much common ground between the Bundesbank and the government on economic objectives', it is precisely because Pöhl knew that this national consensus did not exist in the Community at large that he and the German government insisted on means of enforcing German policies on the economies of the member states.[57] This interdependence of general economic policy with monetary policy has been recognised by the French government as well: one monetary policy means one economic policy. 'The independence of the monetary institution can only be conceived within interdependence with a strong economic government.'[58] Even the original Delors Report made it clear that 'economic and monetary union form two integral parts of a single whole'.[59] Any politically informed Briton knows that two of the most politically controversial issues during the last three years have been monetary issues: exchange rate policy (membership of the ERM) and interest rate policy.[60] In Britain the sensitive matter of mortgage repayments is directly affected by interest rate policy. Far from being a 'technical matter' as one supporter of EMU has claimed,[61] monetary decisions can be 'extremely important economic policy decisions'.[62] Even Sir Leon Brittan, an ardent supporter of EMU, had explained that 'a central bank...can make full employment harder to achieve by taking the wrong decisions'.[63] Of course, if they do, politicians can disclaim responsibility; but ducking responsibility is fatal in a democracy.

If this were not enough, it is clear that control of fiscal policy would also be transferred to the Community level as a result of the rules on budget deficits. Recent Draft Treaties provide for majority voting in the Council of Ministers to determine economic policy, to decide whether a member state is running an 'excessive' budget deficit and to impose the 'appropriate penalties' if necessary.[64] The Germans have argued that these penalties should be economic sanctions against the offending member state, or even exclusion from the Community.[65]

It is clear that any version of monetary union will inevitably reduce national governments and parliaments to the status of charge-capped local authorities.

It is interesting to note that these German demands for greater centrally-imposed discipline, together with their attacks on British plans for currency competition, came in spite of increasing interest in the proposal in France. There is a significant body of opinion behind the idea of competing currencies. It implies discipline by free competition, rather than the discipline by force which the Germans prefer.[66] Giscard d'Éstaing called the hard ecu a 'positive contribution' after a meeting with John Major as Chancellor.[67] More importantly still, the influential Finance Minister, Pierre Bérégovoy, has repeatedly gone out of his way to express interest in the British proposals,[68] emphasising that the French view is closer to the British than to the German.[69]

Despite this, it seems that what is now on offer is not the true independence of monetary policy which would come from free competition between different currencies and policies (whether the currencies remained in the public sector as at present or whether they were in private hands), but instead the imposition of one economic and monetary policy by a powerful and unaccountable institution. It is difficult to think of anything more politically dangerous or undemocratic.

Meanwhile, the federalists try to pretend that this is not happening, or that it will not matter. A frequent tactic is to try to distort the meaning of words. It is a breathtaking tactic and has been used most dramatically in the debate over federalism. When Luxembourg finally admitted what many had been saying for years, that it wants a federal EC, British federalists tried to pretend that the Luxembourgers do not mean federal when they say 'federal'. So it is with sovereignty. There are those who love to confuse the fundamental issue of power by talking about 'legal definitions of sovereignty', claiming that because these are outdated, Westminster should hand over the powers which it does have to Brussels.

It is obvious that sovereignty does not mean dictatorship. Every democratic constitution is based on the limitation of power. In Britain, the sovereignty of Parliament was conceived in opposition to royal absolutism; in the United States the separation of powers limits the government's powers and the constitution is sovereign. It has long been accepted that, even in countries such as these, the field of human rights and the administration of justice are matters in which the government has no right to interfere, and there are even mechanisms where a non-national body may pronounce on national decisions, such as the European Court of Human Rights at Strasbourg.

Neither does sovereignty mean autarky or isolationism. When federalists bleat on about how interdependent the world is, one wonders what world they live in. Britain, like most other countries, has been entering treaties and alliances with other countries for hundreds of years. She has been an ally of Portugal for over 600 years. She is currently a member of scores of international institutions, many of which entail an agreement to act in concert with allies. One thinks of NATO, GATT, the G7, the EC, the Commonwealth, and so on. It is absurd to think that the principle of pooling sovereignty is something new or difficult to accept.

One might distinguish three kinds of policy areas in which a country either is or is not sovereign. In economic policy, for instance, Britain is currently sovereign in that it is the Chancellor of the Exchequer who takes decisions given the circumstances of the day and defends his decisions before Parliament. In NATO, Britain is certainly committed to common aims, and defence policy must often be cleared with NATO allies first. This is because Britain could not have defended herself in the Cold War order, and the common enemy demanded common action. Yet membership of NATO did not prevent Britain's stand during the Falklands or the Gulf. In trade and agriculture, thirdly, Britain is committed always to pursue policies in concert with other EC members, and has pooled sovereignty in these areas completely.

However, there is a fundamental difference between pooling sovereignty on trade and agriculture and pooling economic sovereignty. If a country does not have control over its tax and expenditure, then it cannot be said to have control over anything, since everything comes down to money in the end. Handing over the power to tax and spend means handing over the power to govern. European public expenditure policy, of the kind proposed in successive Community documents, could potentially affect spending on anything from health to education, social services or defence. It is in this sense that EMU would tear the heart out of national parliaments.

It is distressing to see the pro-integrationists trying to muddy the waters. Sir Leon Brittan has tried to argue that the concept of sovereignty is fundamentally archaic and cranky, fit only for medieval speculation.[70] It is surprising, therefore, that the concept should be alive and well in Germany, especially where economic and monetary matters are concerned. The Deutsche Bank described German monetary union thus: 'On July 1st, 1990, the Bundesbank will assume *monetary sovereignty for East Germany.*' Pöhl has said, 'I continue to have substantial doubts whether all or any governments would really be willing to *relinquish the monetary policy sovereignty* of their countries.' Indeed, even on the political level, the German press and public opinion were much preoccupied with the question of national sovereignty at the time of unification. Many Germans, especially on the left, felt that the obligations of NATO membership (which Britain and other members shared) placed an unacceptable restriction on German sovereignty.

Sir Geoffrey Howe has treated the question of sovereignty at some length. In his article 'Sovereignty and interdependence: Britain's place in the world',[71] he defines sovereignty as 'a nation's practical capacity to maximise its influence in the world'[72] and uses the metaphor of a 'bundle of sticks', some of which are exchanged for others, to illustrate that 'sovereignty is not like virginity, something you either have or do not have.' It is difficult not to notice that the 'bundle of sticks' is reminiscent of the Roman *fasces*, the bundle of rods with a protruding axe-head, carried before Roman consuls as a sign of the state authority of Rome, and adopted by Mussolini as a symbol of the movement he led to power in 1922, whence the word 'fascist'.

Those who died while protecting the Lithuanian parliament from Soviet tanks and the 'black beret' crack troops were hardly imagining a great role for Lithuania in world councils: they just wanted their country to run its own affairs without foreign domination, which they have now achieved. The fact that Estonia and the Ukraine have proposed the issue of their own currencies illustrates how the control of tax and expenditure lie at the heart of independent government. The Ukraine determined in October 1991 to have its own 400,000-strong army.

It is certainly true that it is worth 'pooling' sovereignty in some areas since it makes more sense to do this than to act independently. But there is a difference between pooling your sovereignty and drowning it. The supporters of EMU seek to distort reality and confuse the issue, as usual. Sir Leon Brittan tells a famous story of how the Chancellor once raised interest rates half an hour after the Bundesbank, and uses this to illustrate that 'British sovereignty lasted for 30 minutes'. The implication is that sovereignty is not worth having, since we are totally constrained by what the Germans do anyway. In fact, the decision was taken because at the time the government was pursuing a policy of shadowing the Deutsche Mark, a policy which it could be called upon to defend in Parliament. At other times, it has pursued a policy of letting the pound float. These policies are its own. In any case, the dependence on Germany is exaggerated: during 1991 British interest rates have been falling, while German rates have been rising. Certainly we are interdependent, but under EMU we would be totally dependent, for there is a big difference between entering an agreement to keep exchange rates within certain (adjustable) margins and handing over monetary and economic policy control *en bloc*. A country can leave the ERM or change the rate if it wishes. France considered doing the former, and has devalued repeatedly. The difference between the ERM and EMU is the difference between competition between monetary policies and the control of monetary policies. Some suggest that we would all be better off if the Germans controlled our monetary policy and our economy. A defeatist, appeasement-like attitude often lies at the heart of federalist thinking found in some parts of the City of London but is repudiated by those such as Professor Tim Congdon in the *Sunday Telegraph* on 20 October 1991 – 'City's Silly Euro-scare'.

As the House of Lords Select Committee put it, 'It is consistent with the attribute of sovereignty in the international law sense for states to enter into groupings such as alliances or international organisations ...Acceptance of such restraints does not imply loss of sovereign status by individual states. But it is possible that so much competence could be transferred from the member states to the Community that member states would lose their status as sovereign states'.[73] No one should be in any doubt that the intention is to control the economies of the member states. The Draft Treaties for Economic and Monetary Union published at the end of 1990 replace references to 'co-ordination' or 'co-operation' in economic policy with references to 'the institution of a common economic policy...and the implementation of other common policies; the definition and pursuit of a *single* monetary policy...to support the common economic policy.' In the Single European Act of 1986 there is a proviso that 'the institutions of the Community shall take care not to prejudice the internal or external financial stability of the member states'. This article is to be suppressed. As the Intergovernmental Conferences move forward, the gearing becomes more important.

When the Luxembourgers let the cat out of the bag by talking about federalism in June 1991, they were merely reflecting long-term currents of thought in the Community.[74] The objectives of the federalists are to impose ever greater levels of central control. The Luxembourg Draft Treaty said, 'Economic policy instruments will have to be reinforced. The field of economic policy is very wide and cannot be reduced to budgetary policy. The range of instruments to be used goes far beyond those required for simply co-ordinating economic policies.' The Commission's report on EMU speaks of Community competence in 'competition policy, commercial policy, research and technological development, European-wide infrastructure, labour markets, the environment and some aspects of taxation'[75] even though federalism is said not to mean centralisation. Above all, as the Commission says, 'adopting a single currency rather than having national currencies with irrevocably fixed exchange rates would not only have a symbolic character. It constitutes a point of no return.'[76]

People's natural prejudices may be aroused by this prospect alone, sufficiently for the idea to be rejected, but it must be made clear why EMU is undesirable for Britain and for Europe.

There are three scenarios for EMU. The first has effectively been ruled out by the odd admission by the federalists, and has been dealt with earlier. The idea that control of monetary policy can be hived off from the rest of economic policy is false. Monetary policy cannot be given to an 'independent' bank because it makes no sense to talk of monetary policy as independent of economic policy. The idea has effectively been ruled out by the Commission's clear reference to the need for a 'common economic policy', but the myth that it is possible to separate one from the other persists in Britain.[77] The Germans and the French consider it impossible to have a central bank in the EC without binding rules, sanctions and other instruments for imposing economic policy, since 'even an independent central bank cannot ensure price stability alone, as monetary policy does not operate in a vacuum, but rather has close links with other fields'.[78] Because, according to Pöhl, 'monetary policy must not be obstructed by fiscal policy',[79] an 'independent' central bank would not only be completely unprecedented in recent history, it would also represent an immense concentration of power in the hands of unaccountable bankers, who would perforce be implementing policies which might be very unpopular, within an area in which there may well not be the kind of national consensus which obtains in Germany.

Secondly, central bankers, like other human beings, can take the wrong decisions. The central bankers in the US made mistakes in the 1970s, the anti-inflationary Conservative government made mistakes during 1987 and 1988, the Germans made serious mistakes over monetary union in Germany in 1990. What redress is there to be for independent bankers who are to be immune from dismissal and are to have, as Pöhl so quaintly put it, 'adequate financial arrangements during and after their term in office'? Such a solution is highly undemocratic. Of course Parliament in Britain does not control monetary policy on a day-to-day basis, but at least the Chancellor can be called to account for his policies, and he and his government will be judged on their performance. Pöhl has argued that his proposed central banking system 'would have an adequately democratic legal base if it came about by agreement between democratic governments, ratified by democratically elected parliaments, and if the system were provided with a clearly defined mandate'.[80] Such a deeply mistaken belief can only come from a citizen of a country with a disciplinarian attitude to politics. It is the equivalent of a British government refusing to appear for questions in the House saying that it had been elected and therefore did not need to defend its decisions before parliament. The idea of presenting a yearly 'report' to the European Parliament, as the Draft Treaty suggests, is laughably inadequate, since the author of such a report could put what he liked in it.[81] One cannot square the circle of being 'independent and accountable': it will be either one or the other. 'Independence' must be firmly rejected.

The second scenario is that there would be some degree of Community economic policy-making. According to the joint letter issued by President Mitterrand and Chancellor Kohl before the second Rome summit in December 1990, the idea seems to be that this power might rest with the Council of Ministers. 'We propose that, in order to promote the effectiveness of the Union, the role and the tasks of the Council be confirmed and enlarged...Within the Council, majority voting should be the role for all Community matters. Exceptions to this rule should apply only to a limited number of sectors enumerated in the Treaty.'[82] This will include economic policy, asylum policy, the fight against drugs and international crime, and eventually security and foreign policy. It has long been the French preference to maintain the Council as the primary decision-making body of the Community, and indeed to reinforce its role; the Germans want greater powers for the Parliament in Strasbourg. It might seem surprising, then, that Chancellor Kohl should seem to have accepted the French position, until one reflects for a moment on the implications. The idea is a democratic disaster. 'It makes no sense to regard ministers as any longer accountable to their national parliaments for policies on which they have been outvoted in the Council of Ministers. If the voting strength of individual ministers in the Council has been irretrievably weakened through erosion of the veto, this means that control by national parliaments has also been irretrievably weakened'.[83] Not only would national parliaments not have any control over the decisions reached in the Council, no one else would either. The system would resemble nothing so much as the 'democratic centralism' much beloved of Leninist and Maoist governments. It could not survive for long, and the Council would soon have to be made accountable to the European Parliament in some form or another. At that moment, there would be true European government along the lines of a federal superstate.

This leads on to the third scenario, that decisions would be taken in economic and other fields at Community level, and that they would be submitted to the scrutiny of the European Parliament. There are many reasons why this would be bad for democracy.

First, the European Parliament can never be as accountable to the electorate as the national parliaments. The MEPs' constituencies are simply too huge, and they make any true representation of the needs and interests of individual voters impossible. Power would move away from the people, to a remote and opaque institution. The European Parliament is not an institution which excites interest in voters, and the percentage of people who vote in European elections is very low. When they do vote, they usually cast their votes on national issues: Neil Kinnock called for the June 1989 elections to be a judgement on Mrs Thatcher's term in office. Christopher Tugendhat, a former Commissioner, has written of the dreamlike sensation in Brussels, where the daily drama of Community life goes almost entirely unreported in the national newspapers on sale in the city.[84] An MEP has made the point that the Parliament has simply not put down enough roots for it to be realistic to expect it to increase its powers.[85]

Those federalists who make the comparison with the United States ignore the growing body of opinion which supports constitutional reform there (including the idea that Secretaries of State should be cross-examined on the floor of the House, as in Westminster), the chronically low level of participation in elections, and the widespread dissatisfaction with the federal system. The author has recently travelled throughout the USA where it is clear that there is dissatisfaction with the devolution of functions to the states without accompanying funds. Federalism has severe critics in America. Even more astonishingly, the federalists ignore the collapse or near collapse of multi-national federations in other parts of the world, even when these are democratic. Confederations fare no better.

Secondly, democratic parliaments around the world generally try to operate on a two-party basis. In countries where the political history or the voting system produces a myriad of parties, these are nearly always grouped into government and opposition. It is impossible to see how the European Parliament, with its seventy national and political groupings, could ever form coherently enough for true parliamentary debate and opposition to take place. Indeed, the European Parliament is notable for the presence of right-wing and left-wing extremists among its ranks. Countries such as Italy which have neither strong governments nor strong oppositions are noted for the chronic instability of their political systems, and for the fact that power seeps away from the democratic institutions into the bureaucracy or, worse, into organised crime. In Israel, as in Weimar, extremists can gain the balance of power, especially with proportional representation. Parliaments must connect government with the governed, and a significant transfer of power away from national parliaments would represent a weakening of institutions with which people are familiar, and which they can understand, and a strengthening of one which is remote and weak.

Thirdly, these weaknesses are endemic. Parliamentary procedure, like all aspects of political life, is a matter of habit. You cannot create a constitution just by writing on a piece of paper, as the French are so fond of doing. Tradition and practice are essential. The procedures of the European Parliament are weak and shambolic. The committees meet but rarely, they have no effective party divisions, they engage in generalised debate, relying on the work of individual rapporteurs for the purpose of acquiring more federalist powers. Above all, the language barriers render true debate impossible, and they make the workings of the Parliament opaque to the ordinary voter. It is impossible to have a proper exchange of views of the kind which is essential for the true functioning of a parliamentary democracy if everybody is wearing headphones. A taste of things to come was the meeting of 258 national and European parliamentarians in Rome in

November 1990. Some 250 amendments to the final communiqué on European Union were voted on, with no discussion, in a couple of hours, by delegates sitting pressing buttons like robots. It was a tragic farce.

Since the European Parliament can never work as a real parliament, power would pass into the back rooms where intrigue and shabby voting deals are the *modus operandi*. (These remarks are already true of the French and Italian parliaments.) Democracy is not just about having elections: it is about having a proper parliament capable of scrutiny and of holding governments to account. If a parliament cannot effectively question a government, power will slip from its grasp, and government will become autocratic, benign or otherwise.

The most likely result is that neither of these options will prevail and that there will be a kind of fudge. Herein lies the danger: that power will lurk, unspecified and unaccountable, in the shadows of compromise. And where will this power lie? To be frank, when Pöhl says that a single monetary policy will be unable to take into account the needs of individual regions and countries, what he really means is that the policy will be unable to take these into account if they conflict with Germany's needs. Germany, with the strongest economy, will demand policies to maintain that strength, resisting any threat to that pre-eminence in the name of 'Europe'.

The point was made earlier, with reference to the US Federal Reserve, that central bankers are part of a society whose thoughts, opinions and prejudices they inevitably share. This is as true of Germany as anywhere else. Indeed, it is a striking feature of Germany's economic life that there is a strong national consensus between 'the boards of the banks and the large companies (Konzerne) in discreet but effective liaison with the Federal Government and the Länder'.[86] There is a strong 'old boy network' among German banks and industry,[87] and this is reflected in the high degree of control which the German banks exercise over German industry through their shareholdings. This is especially true of the huge Konzerne which are the backbone of the German economy, and between the big three (Deutsche Bank, Dresdener Bank, Commerzbank) there is often a majority of votes on the boards. This comfortable position is encouraged by a close co-operation between the banks (even though there are occasional disagreements[88]). Their intervention in industrial policy is formidable. It was the Deutsche Bank which bought the great and corrupt Flick empire from the family owners before they could restructure it and sell it off in sections: it was Deutsche as well which, within the space of a few years, succeeded in transforming Daimler-Benz into a huge diversified Konzerne, making it the largest in the country, by successively buying the motor company MTU, the aeronautics firm Dornier, the electronics firm AEG and merging them with Messerschmitt Blohm to give birth to an industrial empire of 400,000 employees and £27 billion turnover.[89]

The banks' role in the economy is thus crucial, and this was underlined when Chancellor Kohl turned to them for help in rebuilding East Germany. 'When, one month after German monetary union, East Germany's state run economy showed signs of breaking down on a massive scale, Chancellor Kohl...called in the top bankers of the land. That bankers' summit at the Bonn Chancellery on 8 August 1990 and a similar blue-ribbon meeting on 6 September underscore the important role West Germany's big banks are playing in what some observers call the biggest leveraged buy-out in economic history. With Deutsche and Dresdener leading the pack, the German banks were Kohl's most aggressive support troops on building German monetary and economic union in the marketplace... No wonder that the heads of Deutsche Bank or Dresdener Bank today have the Chancellor's ear':[90] or that it is impossible to acquire German banks.

Moreover, despite initial worries about possible German weakness after reunification,[91] the economic picture now appears more positive.[92] Reunification was the perfect economic takeover for West Germany, which had excess capital to invest and a shortage of skilled labour. Germany is now the largest exporting nation in the world: in the European context she is totally dominant. In the near future, Germany is poised to grow dramatically, profiting more than any other country from the combined boom of 1993 and the new markets to the East. Her GNP will exceed $2 trillion by 1997 and may reach $3 trillion by the year 2000.[93]

By sheer political and economic weight, she would be able to exert sufficient influence on countries economically dependent on her to be sure of dominating majority voting, or by refusing to accept certain policies. These trends have already been apparent in the formulation of the terms for EMU and political union. If it ever came to making hard choices over monetary policy or economic policy where the needs of one region or country conflicted with those of Germany, it is fanciful to think that her priorities, as the self-styled 'motor' of Europe, would not prevail.

4

European Politics and the Drive towards Federalism

They are fighting for their enslavement as if it were a question of their salvation.

Baruch Spinoza, *Tractatus Theologico-politicus.*

Abbé Sieyès has whole nests of pigeon-holes full of constitutions ready made, ticketed, sorted, and numbered; suited to every season and every fancy; some with the top of the pattern at the bottom, and some with the bottom at the top; some plain, some flowered, some distinguished for their simplicity, others for their complexity; some with councils of elders, and councils of youngsters; some without any council at all. Some where the electors choose the representatives; others where the representatives choose the electors.

Edmund Burke, *Letter to a Noble Lord.*

One of the most baffling phenomena in the debate about Europe is that Britain seems to be the only country worried about national sovereignty. The other countries of the EC, which count among their number some of the oldest political units in the world (France, Denmark, the Netherlands, Spain, Portugal), by contrast, seem quite happy to dissolve their sovereignty in the supranationalism of the EC. The transfer of power represented by the adoption of a single currency is a decisive compromise of economic self-government.[1] It has been a tactic of both supporters and opponents of economic and monetary union to play down the significance of these proposals, the first saying that monetary union will not significantly compromise sovereignty, the others sometimes dismissing talk of European union as nothing more than Euro-waffle.[2] While it is true that the terms of the debate are often unclear, and while confusing signs constantly come even from the Euro-enthusiasts (such as when the French Foreign Minister called for 'une fédération d'Etats souverains',[3] the overwhelming evidence indicates that the prime movers in European union mean business.[4] This chapter will try to explain the motives behind these trends, and why the federalists are to be taken seriously.

It should be clear to most people that the Franco-German axis is the main initiator of these plans. For both countries, the special relationship between them is their primary foreign policy priority, and the European Community remains principally an instrument of their foreign policy needs. Before going on to examine the Franco-German relationship and the German Question in the next chapter, however, it is worth asking what it is about Britain that makes it so sensitive over national sovereignty.

The London correspondent of the Russian newspaper, *Literaturnaya Gazeta*, recently put the matter in a nutshell:

> European integration will weaken the British parliamentary system. For Italy or France this is of no particular significance, since the role of their parliaments is not great, but Britain would be depriving itself of its most important political institution.[5]

The questions about European integration are the classic questions about any form of government: how do we want to be governed? Who by? What for?

Ever since Lord Bryce wrote his seminal work in the 1950s on the decline of the legislature in modern democracies, it has become a casual article of faith that parliaments, including Westminster, have become ever more supine in the face of all-powerful governments. Moreover Europeanism is often the consequence of dissatisfaction with one's own political system, a rather defeatist, not to say appeasement-like, attitude which often displays what one commentator has called 'a peculiar combination of self righteousness and self hatred'.[6] Political culture in mainland European countries is often marked by sheer apathy and disinterest, and plans for European union exploit this. In Britain the hostility of some to British political life is more explicit, with the implicit suggestion that we ought to solve our problems by handing over our powers of self government to those clever foreigners instead. One thinks of Paddy Ashdown's remark that Britain is the most undemocratic country in Europe. One might forgive the hyperbole in a politician but it is less easy to take from academic or journalistic critics. Typical is William Wallace of St Antony's College, Oxford:

> [the anti-federalists] use arguments of 30 years ago against constitutional entanglement with the Continent. Dare any Conservative MEP explain how all this looks to political leaders on the Continent? The passion with

> which the mythology of parliamentary sovereignty is defended... baffles Paris and Bonn. They see an outdated institution, with an unrepresentative electoral base, through which government proposals pass easily with little amendment into law.[7]

It is possibly true of 'Bonn': Germany has a long tradition of unease about England, which has been kept alive and well in influential papers such as *Die Zeit* and elsewhere.[8] The author recalls a visit to the German Bundestag where the British were roundly berated for being 'little Englanders'. It was interesting that at the controversial Chequers seminar on Germany six British and American experts voiced overwhelmingly favourable opinions about Germany and the Germans ('If Chancellor Kohl had sat in, he would have agreed with or accepted as fair comments 90 per cent of what was said', commented one of them[9]). But when BBC 2's 'Newsnight' organised a kind of return match four German historians and journalists dwelt long on Britain's archaic society and nineteenth-century delusions of grandeur. However, Wallace's remark is highly improbable as an account of opinion in France, given the overwhelming sense of crisis in the political life of that country. One even comes across the occasional flattering remarks in the French press,[10] which shows that there are a number of people in France, and not just Gaullists, who understand the British defence of their parliamentary sovereignty quite well.

But the argument must stand or fall on its merits. What is a parliament for? How do the constitutional procedures and general political procedures in the other countries of the EC compare and what do these differences tell us about their attitudes to European integration? Would it be better or worse for democracy if significant powers were transferred to the European level, away from national parliamentary control? Such questions are hardly, as some would say, 'piffle'.[11]

While political science has greatly concentrated on the role of governments and the executive, at the cost of examining the role of legislatures, it is clear that academic comment now presents a more varied picture of the role of parliaments than that of the decline of which Lord Bryce wrote.[12] To begin with, parliaments have never governed, as the history of Westminster proves:

> At no time in its long history of seven hundred years has Parliament governed, nor save for a brief period when the Constitution broke down in the seventeenth century has it made any claim to do so. Parliament's role has not been executive, but supervisory – it has sought to subject the executive to certain limits and controls, to protect the liberties of the individual citizen against the arbitrary use of power, to focus the mind of the nation on the great issues of the day by the maintenance of a

> continuous dialogue or discussion, and by remaining at the centre of the stage to impose...'manners of behaviour' on the whole political system. Of course, all this presupposes information as to what is happening. The more important the issue, the greater the information must be. After all, members of the Cabinet are also Members of Parliament.
>
> The Commons, by its elected status, associates the people with the government, and thus makes a major contribution to legitimacy, a concept essential for government by consent. It provides continuity, not by the imposition of the rule of a single class or caste, but by furnishing a means by which power can pass peacefully from one class to another without the upheaval or disorder of revolution. It further ensures the reality of government by consent by bringing governors and the governed into close relationship and enabling the views of citizens to reach their rulers and vice versa...The first function of the Commons is still to sustain an effective government.[13]

This elegant summary serves as a useful description of what the functions of a parliament should be, even though the text in question is specifically about Westminster. The sting is in the tail. Those who bemoan the weakening of the governmental role of parliaments are not only failing to bear English history in mind where Parliament never had that role, they are forgetting continental history as well. One of the fundamental principles on which the present day French and German constitutions are based, as will be seen later, is the need to preserve governmental stability and executive initiative in the day-to-day running of government. The IIIrd and IVth Republics in France collapsed because of their chronic instability: the average life of a cabinet in the IVth Republic was less than seven months, while under the IIIrd Republic it had been nine.[14] The Weimar Republic suffered the same fate: 'not only the total triumph of Hitler, but also the more moderate anti-parliamentarians of de Gaulle can be attributed in no small degree to malaise about the discontinuity in the politics of parliamentary governments'.[15]

Parliament must perform what political scientists call 'regime support systems': that is, the parliamentary process confers authority upon governmental activity and law making. To be sure, parliament is not the only source of authority: elections have become more and more highly valued as its main source. Yet it is arguable that it is the central question about any political system whether the decision making process, the institutions and the political culture which obtains, confer a sufficient degree of authority on the decisions themselves and upon those in power that those same institutions are still respected even if, in individual cases, the decisions themselves are not; for lack of authority within a system and the respect this conveys can have catastrophic results.[16]

A parliament must connect the government with the governed.

There must be a direct line of accountability from the man in the street, via his MP who is accountable to his constituents, to the minister who takes part in the Council of Ministers and the government, who are accountable to parliament. Parliament must be the primary place where the conflicting claims and interests of society can be articulated and resolved. This is achieved by debates and the questioning of ministers and in committees. As a legislative body, a parliament will be judged on its ability to hold decision-makers to account, to render government transparent, and thoroughly to scrutinise both legislative proposals and the non-legislative activities of government departments. It should be able to rectify or modify legislation, and in some cases should be able to initiate it. In short, a parliament must both support and supervise government, while at the same time maintaining itself as the focus of political debate and, above all, as the instrument for political change, by offering the electorate a credible alternative government. Moreover, a parliament will benefit from a thriving political culture and critical scrutiny and debate in the media and, conversely, suffer from public apathy. This was the case in the Weimar Republic, where the parliament, although endowed with strong formal powers, was vulnerable because it lacked public support.[17] A final threat to parliamentary government is increasing technocracy: 'the modern state in all advanced countries has become a formidable machine of which the control lies less in the hands of elected representatives of the people than of technicians, specialists, experts. The era of a techno-structure or of technocracy has as a corollary the decline of the powers of parliamentary democracy in the true sense'.[18]

How do other countries of the EC meet these criteria?

To begin with France, it is clear that there are serious problems both in the country's political culture and in the constitution and that the French are aware of this. Indeed, it is hard to exaggerate the sense of crisis which currently prevails in French political life.[19] It is true that the French are prone to see things in rather sombre terms: it suits their sense of drama. In 1909 Jules Michelet spoke of a crisis in 'La démocratie en France'. Some of the causes of the crisis are familiar to other countries (although it is typical of the little Englander approach of the federalists in Britain that they assume that Britain's problems are unique to her). The abysmal state of the French state education system provoked demonstrations, riots and eventual crisis talks with the government in November 1990. Urban riots and the life of desolation in the *banlieues* (the equivalent of our 'inner cities') produce a sense of moral collapse in French society.[20] The sight of judges and magistrates going on strike and scuffling with police outside the Palace of Justice and the recent murder of a policewoman in a riot (June 1991), as well as the regular disruption of life by numerous strikes, especially in public services, indicate that there is something seriously wrong. Two recent cases of young Arabs dying while in police custody (one of whom fell out of a window while being interrogated) have added to this impression.

However, the crisis is not simply a product of specific policy failures, or of weariness with ten years of Mitterrand. It is perceived to be a crisis of the very institutions of the Vth Republic themselves.

The most un-British element in this is the charge of corruption in the political class. Not confined to France, corruption corrodes public confidence in a political system whenever it appears. The man in the street accepts that all French politicians are in it together and, as a result, charges of corruption seem not to be followed up, even when they are as spectacular as the current scandal concerning the dirty financing of President Mitterrand's election campaign in 1988.[21] The present Minister of Justice, Henri Nallet, was Treasurer of the Socialist Party at the time of the campaign.

Part of the problem is no doubt cultural tradition: a significant factor, however, must also be the strongly localistic flavour in French politics. France enjoys an attitude to local government which is the very opposite of the worst excesses of British local government. Rather than declaring nuclear-free zones or criticising Chile, French local politicians (who are often also national politicians) are judged very much on their performance at local level in delivering services. This attitude is certainly not without advantages, and many might rightly wish it for Britain: however, the favouritist or clientilist pressures are strong. Indeed, 46% of letters written to French *deputés* are to obtain favours: 'promotions, jobs, tax reductions, favourable examination results, telephone installations'.[22] These requests (except perhaps the ones for favourable examination results) are passed on to the local prefecture, and the *deputé* has to show that he can deliver the goods.

While French opinion may thus favour the work at local level of the individual *deputé*, national politics and the Assemblée Nationale are regarded with considerable scepticism, apathy or even contempt. By-elections are marked by spectacularly low turnouts, sometimes less than 30%.[23] Over 60% of French people think that politicians are not interested in what people think.[24] A group of socialist *deputés* recently declared, 'our system is dying in front of our eyes'.[25] Academic commentators have written of 'the current political malaise, electoral abstentionism, the rise of the power of national populism embodied by the National Front, scepticism of the elites, the loss of a general civic spirit, a disenchantment with the world.'[26]

The President of the National Assembly and former Prime Minister,

Laurent Fabius, has spoken of 'the general crisis of politics...the malaise of a society which has lost all its landmarks translates itself into a suspicion of political parties and into a rise of anti-parliamentarianism'.[27] Frankly admitting that 'parliament is no longer the centre of power that it was', he points out that the only political orator left in France is Le Pen, who is not a *deputé*.[28] Moreover, Le Pen's party, despite a professed desire to rejuvenate French politics, has done more to make it absurd than any other, quite apart from the base populist ideas which it propagates. On the infamous 'night of the long keys' National Front *deputés*, finding the chamber empty as usual, rushed around all the empty desks switching the keys left in the voting machines, registering a massive vote in their favour (which was subsequently declared null and void).[29] If nothing else, this absurd event illustrates one thing: that the voting system in the Assemblée Nationale is nearly always done in party blocs by proxy (one or two members are delegated to vote for the whole party). It is difficult to think what could make the Assemblée resemble a rubber stamp more than this.

Anti-parliamentarianism has a long history in France. 'Unlike our British neighbours...the parliamentary system never really established itself in our political life'.[30] This anti-parliamentarianism can come in three forms, from all sides of the political spectrum. On the right, demands are made for the parliament to be overruled in the name of order and authority. Michel Debré, a Prime Minister under de Gaulle and author of the constitution of the Vth Republic, declared that 'since in France government stability cannot come from the electoral law, it must come from making governmental rules',[31] a classic statement justifying *raison d'état* and distrust of the people. On the left there is the Jacobin tradition, which draws on the Rousseauist doctrine of the general will, expressed thus by Robespierre: 'Wherever the people does not exercise its authority and does not manifest its power itself, but only through representatives and if the representative body is not pure and identified with the people, then liberty is extinguished.' The third course of anti-parliamentarianism is neither the authoritarianism and distrust of political parties of the right (although President Mitterrand also seems to share it[32]), nor the belief in direct democracy of the left, but is an unsystematic belief that the actual people running the country are useless. 'It is the most common form, an anti-parliamentarianism of crisis, a sudden flame of protest against the cronies who govern us, a deep desire, which come from a desperate belief that "things must change".'[33] This is the kind of growing resentment which obtains in France, and which Le Pen exploits and fosters.

The Vth Republic is the embodiment of the second of two choices which French constitutions have made: on the one hand, an emphasis upon government accountable to France's traditionally very fragmented and non-consensual society, at the expense of 'order and future goals'; and on the other, an emphasis on order and future goals at the expense of parliamentary representation and accountability.[34] This is the meaning of de Gaulle's exasperated remark, 'How can one govern a country which makes 400 different types of cheese?' The constitution of the Vth Republic was intended to overcome the chronic factionalism, irresponsibility and opportunism which characterised the behaviour of *deputés* under those republics, and which rendered the government inoperable. (There is an illuminating analogy with the Italian constitution of our own days.) The legislature, both the Assembly and the Senate, enjoyed huge powers of death by committee and were easily able to bring down governments, which resulted in the inevitable instability. In addition to generating a mistrust of politics and political parties, this had another effect – the rise of the bureaucrat. During the IVth Republic France was not governed, she was administered. The government of the day carried through the efforts of the most highly trained and intelligent of any group of civil servants in continental Europe. Neither the Monnet plan, nor the 2nd, 3rd and 4th economic plans were ever effectively debated by the Assembly. They were largely the work of anonymous bureaucrats.[35]

De Gaulle's suspicion of political parties was explicitly anti-parliamentarian: 'it is from the head of state, placed above parties and elected more widely than just by Parliament that executive power must proceed'.[36] This suspicion of parties has left its mark on the names of the right-wing parties in France: his successors' party is called 'Rassemblement pour la République', the word 'rassemblement' (rally) connecting a wide popular extra-parliamentary movement. The same might be said of Giscard d'Estaing's less populist party, the 'Union pour la Democratie Française'. These attitudes are in striking contrast to the British tradition, where party conflict is the primary institutional feature of Westminster and has been for over a century.

The historical legacy of this suspicion of parliamentary government is nowhere clearer than in the constitution of the Vth Republic, and an examination of this will show how, with partial replacement of national by EC government, different countries have different things to lose.

People in Britain are often aware of French centralism and of the power of the President. Both these are sometimes slightly exaggerated: there has been some decentralisation since 1983 and, as the period of cohabitation demonstrated, the President's power can be compromised if he is faced by a hostile majority in the Assemblée Nationale. None the less, the President presides over the Conseil des Ministres (the Cabinet) and is responsible for determining the main outlines of policy while reserving certain areas almost exclusively for himself (especially defence and foreign policy). M. Giscard d'Estaing considered that economic policy was his domain as well.[37] When Michel Rocard was replaced by Edith Cresson on 15 May 1991, his official letter of resignation made it clear that President Mitterrand had asked him to resign, even though the constitution does not give him the right (the President is responsible for 'nominating' the Prime Minister and for approving the Cabinet, but not for dismissing him). Mme Cresson's first speech in the Assemblée Nationale as Prime Minister made it clear that the President had asked her to form a government for specific policy objectives, defined by him, and Mitterrand underlined this himself in his broadcast to the nation the night of the change of government. He enjoys this power without any accountability to parliament, of course: once elected he remains in office for seven years without ever having to justify his policies to anyone except via the media, and interviews to the Head of State are usually rather tame and grovelling. Indeed these immense powers were once criticised sharply in a pamphlet entitled 'The Permanent Coup d'Etat' by a young socialist *deputé* in the 1960s, François Mitterrand.[38]

Even more astonishing are the powers accorded to the government as a whole, for it is here that the primacy of the executive over the legislature is most clear. The power of the government is positively breathtaking in comparison with that of ministers in Westminster: 'the French parliament in the Vth Republic is modest to the point of being inadequate...Its most serious short-comings are its failure to be seen as an arena for national debate...and its incapacity to be a check on executive power'.[39]

29 of the 89 articles of the constitution deal with limitations on the parliament's power and ways in which the government can restrict it. The parliament cannot sit for more than six months of the year (Article 28); the agenda is entirely determined by the government, its legislative duties are restricted to a specific range of policy areas (Article 34) and its ability to hold ministers to account and to scrutinise and amend legislation is pitifully small. Its only real weapon over the government is that it can propose a vote of censure. If this is passed the government falls: however, despite the fact that such motions are debated every few months, only one has succeeded since the constitution was drawn up in 1958. In terms of day-to-day influence over policy or even in terms of control over the executive, its powers are risible. It cannot even decide its own procedures (and has been prevented from so doing by the Conseil Constitutionel).

One commentator writes:

> There is complete executive supremacy in the legislative process, severely limited opportunities for general debates criticising the government, virtually no opportunities for scrutinising executive acts and making the executive give an account of them...Executive power is a little too immune from proper scrutiny...The democrat looks to a parliament to ensure that the executive is kept under scrutiny and prevented from abusing its powers. Questions, debates, committee hearings, parliamentary procedure for removing the executive from power – these are the usual means for doing this. There are many ways in which governments and their supporters can prevent these methods from being effective, but they cannot work at all if the opposition has no real procedural opportunity to apply real scrutiny, nor if its efforts do not arouse the media of information and public opinion. This is the real problem in France.[40]

The details of French parliamentary procedure confirm this. There are no opposition days and no emergency debates. There are only debates on ministerial statements and these are not followed by a vote: in any case such statements are rare. The Rocard government made only one in 1988, there were 16 between 1973 and 1978 and only 14 during the socialist government of 1981 to 1986. Articles 45 and 48 give priority to government *projets de loi* (bills) and allow the government to intervene in the *navette* (when legislation shuffles back and forth) between the Assemblée and the Senate, overruling the latter. Article 44 states, 'If the government requires, the Assembly must pronounce with a single vote on the whole or part of the text in question making only those amendments accepted by the government', which enables the government to bypass the scrutiny procedures (such as they are) entirely. It is the equivalent of a bill becoming law after the Second Reading. (It is frequently used: Chirac used it 22 times in 1987; it was used 43 times between 1986 and 1988.) The infamous Article 49.3 allows the government to declare a bill a matter of confidence, in which case no further debate on it is permitted and the bill is automatically adopted unless a motion of no confidence is tabled and passed within two days. This measure was used twelve times by Raymond Barre (1978 to 1981); ten times under Mauroy and Fabius (1981 to 1966); seven times in 1986 alone (Chirac). It was used in 1979 (Barre) and 1989 (Rocard) to pass Finance Bills, for laws on prices and incomes (1982), for laws on press freedom (1984) and for laws on the Health Service (1991). Article 38 permits the government to rule by decree. Chirac used this (1986-88) for a series of economic and social measures, including privatisation and for a reform of the electoral law in 1986.[41] This is in addition to the powers to rule by decree as a result of the circumscription of parliament's areas of competence (Article 34). The committee system is woefully inadequate. There are only six permanent legislative committees, whose membership is far too large for any real scrutiny to take place. Laurent Fabius has bemoaned the fact that *deputés* are usually excluded from policy-making committee.[42] Committees of enquiry can be set up ad hoc to look into particular matters, but a government can always prevent one being set up if it fears that the results may be embarrassing, since a majority of the Assemblée must vote for their creation. As most such requests are refused, when they are set up they are usually convened only to discuss matters of specific interest, such as the textile industry or the state of the French language. If they ever do reveal controversial findings, as occasionally happens if a government sets up a committee to examine the activities of its predecessor, the report often merits little more attention that a small paragraph in *Le Monde*.

Finally, the government seems to have got into the habit of treating the Assemblée Nationale with some contempt. The Minister for Relations with Parliament, Jean Poperen, reported in December 1990 that over 2,000 parliamentary questions put to the government up to six months previously remained unanswered. Over 800 questions remained unanswered for a year, 500 for eighteen months and near 400 questions were still unanswered after two years. In theory all parliamentary questions must be answered after one month. In Westminster they take much less time.[43]

This leads on to the question of political culture. Perhaps as a result of the weakness of the French parliament, there is little sense of popular day-to-day involvement in politics. Instead apathy reigns, not least among the young, even students. There is little public interest in the business of politics and a good deal of contempt for the political process and the political class. Radio and television programmes of the high inquiring calibre of 'Today', 'The World at One' or 'Newsnight' do not exist in France to anything like the same degree.[44] Nowhere is this clearer than in the debate about Europe, or rather in its absence. While the British are agonising over their future choices in Europe, Europe is hardly ever discussed in France. At the time of the second Rome summit in December 1990 there was saturation coverage in Britain of John Major's first appearance at a European summit as Prime Minister. Whole programmes of 'Today' and 'The World Tonight' were devoted to it: the BBC called it 'this historic summit'. By an almost unbelievable contrast, the summit was not even mentioned on the main 8 pm television news in France (Antenne 2), although it did get a ten second slot as the tenth item on the midnight news bulletin. European summits are usually mentioned in the *Diplomatie* columns of *Le Monde*, but this reinforces the impression that Europe does not concern domestic politics. Debates on Europe in the Assemblée Nationale are attended by a mere handful of *deputés* and after the dramatic debate in Westminster in June 1991, Jacques Delors remarked that only the British were discussing Europe properly, adding that he wished the other countries would do the same.[45] It is an interesting question what the French will do with Article 3 of the 'Declaration of the Rights of Man and the Citizen' if a treaty of European Union were ever adopted: 'The principle of all sovereignty resides necessarily in the Nation. No body, no individual may exercise authority which does not expressly emanate from the Nation.' If such a treaty were signed, it will be less a result of any great Europeanism in France and more the result of a fit of absence of mind.

Could it be that Europeanism is in direct proportion to dissatisfaction with one's own political institutions? Douglas Hurd remarked at one summit that 'some of the other member states have less faith in their own institutions than we do'.[46] The British Parliament depends on a direct constituency link. A German Ambassador once remarked to the author at a conference that he had referred several times to his constituents, 'whereas we in Germany believe in institutions'. Certainly, if your constitutional arrangements are recent, you might feel more disposed to abandon them and draw up some new ones instead. France has had seventeen constitutions since 1789 and, as the figure suggests, seems rather to enjoy drawing up new ones. Germany, Spain, Greece, Portugal and Italy have all been dictatorships in the last fifty years, some of them recently. The present governmental arrangements of some countries provide their inhabitants with reasons to replace their government with European government, because they claim it will be better. 'Greece strongly supports a stronger role for the European Parliament, although it only has 24 seats. The parliament is popular, and Greece's domestic political situation will teach lessons in stability and procedure to the national parliament.'[47] The threat of economic collapse, a government (Papandreou's) which ended in a welter of corruption of the most Balkan variety and a very recent history of dictatorship certainly make Brussels preferable to Athens for many Greeks. Spain and Portugal, although both ancient nation states, associate 'Europe' with the end of dictatorship and, no doubt, subsidies.

Belgium is the extreme case of a country whose own institutions are so weak that EC integration seems the only substitute. The attitude to the Belgian state within that country can perhaps be illustrated by an anecdote. In the federal parliament a Walloon *deputé* asks a parliamentary question about the nationality of staff in a government department, eager to establish that there is a fair balance. The minister responsible gives the figures as follows: 'Out of fifty employees, twenty-five are Flemish, twenty-four are Walloon and one is Belgian.' The *deputé*, in a supplementary question, asks what on earth the minister means by 'Belgian' and demands that he clarify this category which he says he does not recognise. The minister duly does so and reports to the House that the Belgian is a Polish immigrant. There have been claims that the division of the state into three federal regions following the nationalist violence and other crises has seriously damaged the Belgian state and constitution. 'It seems there is no longer a state of Belgium... The central state is rapidly disappearing. Now, all of sudden, my concern is that there will be no state left, and no nation either', remarked one commentator.[48]

Italy shares some of the problems of Belgium and Greece. The former Prime Minister, Emilio Colombo, has remarked that he wants European integration to occur in order to prevent Italy from collapsing into anarchy.[49] The opinion is widespread in Italy that European government would be more efficient than Italy's own slow and corrupt system.[50]

Italy is famous for the instability of her governments. She has had fifty governments since the end of the war, many of them dominated by the same personalities and the same political party. (Giulio Andreotti has been a senior minister since the 1960s). This means that the average life of a government is eleven months. The shortest government ever was that of the great European federalist, Alcide de Gasperi, whose government lasted for twelve days in July 1953. Flush from his success at national level, he decided to turn his prodigious talents to European politics.

This situation is the result of a chronic constitutional impasse in which the government and the parliament have been unable to develop a stable and effective working relationship, because of 'an unreformed public administration, a loosely worded constitution and an unbalanced party political development'.[51] As in France, there are cultural as well as structural problems: the weakness of policy debate and the public sense of alienation from the bizarre workings of their political system mean that the successive crises seldom have anything to do with the outside world. The voting system means that voters see hardly any correlation with the election results and the governments they produce, as the recent crisis in April 1991 showed.[52] Nor is vigorous participation in the parliamentary process encouraged by the need for members of the parliament to build up personal networks of connections to advance their careers.

Unlike France, however, the parliament is not constitutionally supine; indeed it has a degree of control over policy which some might envy, although this is more a result of governmental weakness than anything else. 'In a political system where the processes of government formation and dissolution are often lengthy and byzantine, parliament

...is an instrument of last resort, not a household tool.'[53] In such conditions power slips away from parliament, either into the hands of criminal organisations who control huge sections of the economy or into the hands of powerful industrialists.[54]

The German attitude to Europe will be discussed in depth in the next chapter, but her constitution is worth examining here. Ever since the Swiss Germanist, Fritz Allemann, declared 'Bonn is not Weimar', the Federal Republic's democracy has, generally speaking, enjoyed relatively high support. With memories of the inept and unstable parliamentary experiment under Weimar still fresh, the imperative after the war was to create a stable system. This soon led to criticism of the excessive power of the Chancellor: 'The Chancellor's position has become so strong that his opponents and supporters alike complain about his authoritarian style of leadership [writing about Adenauer] ...Essentially, the regime is demi-authoritarian...Apart from general elections every four years there is no effective means to supervise the government'.[55]

Others have drawn attention to the weak political culture: 'I perceive the most significant structural defect of our democracy in the lethargy and apathy which are increasingly to be found within our parties and other groups...The unease of the Chancellor-democracy is not only a protest at the executive power of the head of the government, but is also a hidden criticism of the opposition, which all too often fails to offer an alternative.'[56]

If there are structural weaknesses in the German constitution and German political life, they perhaps lie halfway between these two remarks, namely that there is an excessive domination of the parties in the political process who fail to bring political discussion sufficiently into the open and consequently do not always offer the electorate a real choice. As in France, there is a strong tendency to run the country like a vast bureaucracy.

To begin with the efficacy of parliamentary control, it is clear that it suffers from the federal constitution itself: the intricacy of policy decisions, complex inter-governmental decision-making structures at the national, sub-national and supranational level, and the inherent complexity of new policy areas, have all made parliamentary scrutiny more difficult. Furthermore, the bureaucracy enjoys significant powers at the expense of the Bundestag. 'The 519 members of the Bundestag cannot rival the expertise and available manhours of federal and *Länder* bureaucracies. This gap in expertise reduces the capability, at least of opposition members, to scrutinise government activities effectively.'[57] It is ironic that theories of federalism, especially of the German variety, should stress responsibility so strongly while failing to realise it in practice. The primacy of the bureaucracy has historical roots (like France): 'In Germany and Prussia the bureaucracy already performed the political policy of function of policy development more than 200 years ago, from the latter part of the eighteenth century onwards, high civil servants were virtually the ruling state.'[58]

Bracher makes the point that the presence of a powerful bureaucracy is intentional:

> In the Federal Republic, the 'chancellor-democracy' has at its disposal a continually growing government and management expertise which outlasts all parliaments: the twenty year long permanence of this government constellation is modified only by the federal structure. Here too the danger of government instability was exchanged for a limitation on the power of government...In the cases of France and Germany, if in different ways, the consequence is a technological-bureaucratic, potentially authoritarian remodelling of parliamentary democracy...By this development, the representation and participation of the citizens was increasingly weakend and 'mediated'...[59]

This weakness of central parliamentary control is in spite of the fact that decisions on tax are taken centrally for the whole country and the revenues are then distributed among the *Länder*.

As a result of the opaqueness of German government, much decision-making and debate takes place within the governing political parties and not in the parliamentary domain. This tendency is strengthened by the institution of the political civil servant. He is a special category of senior civil servant whom a minister can send into temporary retirement and replace with another if he is not felt to share the minister's party political affiliation. The most senior of these officials appear in the Bundestag: oral questions are often answered by the *Staatssekretär* rather than by the minister himself, leading to a weakening of the institution of the oral parliamentary question, especially since the answers given are often not informative or satisfactory, and the length of questions limited.[60]

There is an excessively consensual relationship between the parties, accompanied by a significant degree of intra-party bargaining (within coalitions), away from the glare of parliamentary scrutiny.[61] 'The concessions made by Cabinet ministers in private consultations with government backbenchers are no substitute for public scrutiny.'[62] There are of course parliamentary questions, although individual members of the Bundestag may only ask *Kleine Anfragen* (small questions): a quorum of 26 is need to ask a *Grosse Anfrage* (major question) and these require a fuller reply. There is a kind of Cabinet question time (*Kabinettsbefragung*) but it is not especially popular: most members' work is taken up largely with committee work.

However, one cannot conclude that the committees have a sufficiently important role either:

> Departmental committees do not have autonomous deicison making powers...the vast majority of amendments are of minor importance and the major ones are usually initiated by the government or the Bundesrat (the Council of Länder Ministers). Parties' positions are usually determined beforehand within their working groups or in plenary sessions.[63]

The limits within which committees may modify government proposals are fixed by the major parties. Committee reports are usually adopted without debate by the plenum of the Bundestag. Once again, the bureaucratic-administrative character of German government explains this: both party and Bundestag committees tend to be dominated by experts. This is especially true of the agriculture committee where over three-quarters of the members are from an agricultural background and thus represent agricultural interests. 'The concentration of expertise and interest (in the committees) mean that it is both rare and difficult for someone outside the relevant committee or committees to counter a report'.[64] Where the European issue is concerned, the weakness of this overly consensual approach is underlined by the fact that the Foreign Affairs committee (which has a sub-committee on European affairs) takes its instructions from the Foreign Ministry.

Voting discipline is very high and there is a significant degree of cohesion. Votes are taken anonymously, as is the continental tradition, by a show of hands. Rather than having division lists, the official records merely report 'passed', 'defeated' or 'passed with a few abstentions'. The Bundestag does not initiate legislation and government proposals are hardly ever defeated on the floor of the house. The fact that half of the members of the Bundestag are selected from party lists, rather than being elected, only reinforces the power of the parties, weakens accountability and is open to the usual favouritist pressures. In a long and bitter attack on the political system in Germany, one commentator has drawn attention to the questionable practices which arise from a system in which parties are subsidised by the state, a practice justified by the need to have strong parties in order to maintain a healthy political culture:

> This moderate explanation is the nub for the fatal privilege of the parties...They monopolise access to public positions, they hold competition in check, they allow their expenses to be more than comfortably met from tax revenue and whenever things get tough they form an excessively large coalition, not against any parliamentary minority but

> instead against the majority of non-organised voters...The excessively close links between the civil service and the parties is the main cause of the lack of direction in our political life. Above all the parties have failed in the task of presenting clear alternatives to the questions of the day and thus of deciding them by public debate...They have developed into an oligarchy, most interested in their own affairs...Anybody who has followed the actions of the opposition in Bremen or Hamburg in recent years can hardly avoid the conclusion that the Christian Democrats (the opposition) are not interested in gaining power (since lucrative public positions are given to them anyway)... It was not very difficult for old party hacks from East Germany, like Gysi (the leader of the reformed Communist party, the Party for Democratic Socialism) or Modrow (the former Prime Minister of East Germany, also Communist) to adapt to these practices...Being professionally close to power creates a close bond between politicians as different as Franz-Joseph Strauss (the late conservative Prime Minister of Bavaria) and Schalk-Golodkowski (the disgraced former Communist Finance Minister of East Germany), which is seldom equalled by public allegiances to supposed Christian Democratic or Social Democratic principles.[65]

While this consensual attitude is certainly of enormous benefit when it comes to wage bargaining, it is of less value in politics. In particular, the image of Germany epitomised by her most famous export, the Mercedes, as a country which is well built, reliable, and which performs well, should not blind us to the fact that the history of the Federal Republic has been a history of scandals, which have reached to the very highest echelons of power. The current leader of the small but powerful centre party, the Free Democrats, Count Otto Lambsdorff, is one of the three most powerful men in the government coalition. He was indicted in 1983 for having helped the Flick company escape tax obligations while he was Economics Minister (Flick was a donor to party funds). One also thinks of the suicide of the State Premier, Uwe Barschel. Recently, the Treuhandanstalt, the government department responsible for selling off East German industry, was at the centre of a scandal as its officials were found to have been pocketing the proceeds.[66]

Nor indeed is the famous social market economy without blemishes. The problem in Britain is that the federalists and the press generally, seem to think that everything is bad in Britain while everything is good on the Continent. While Germany spends 40% of her tax revenue on social security, Germans have been dismayed to observe a significant increase in homelessness and destitution on the streets of her cities, especially the rich western cities like Stuttgart and Munich. This is a phenomenon familiar to Londoners and Parisians. Charities for the homeless report that 5,000 new people a year arrive on the streets and that the total figure now stands at a staggering 300,000 for the whole country.[67]

As Ernst Fraenkel observed in 1964:

> If the belief becomes current in public opinion that in the arguments between government and opposition it is not really a matter of opposing opinions being presented, then the impression will increasingly gain currency that parliamentary discussions are just a game. If political groups and parties atrophy into a façade behind which there hides nothing but the power struggles of bureaucrats in the party apparatus, then a pluralist, democratic society will be transformed into a mass of isolated individuals whose political thinking is uniformly directed by the mass media...In the Federal Republic this hollowness of the political parties is already evident in their largely successful attempts to make parties the beneficiaries of the state and members of parliament state employees. As Hannah Arendt has shown, in times of crisis the existence of a formless mass can become the basis for a totalitarian dictatorship; in times of prosperity it can lead to an all-encompassing smugness and self-satisfaction and to the existence of a regime which knows no criticism, no control and, above all, no real opposition and thus no arguments which contain alternatives.[68]

How does Westminster compare to all this? Those hostile to excessive party discipline in Westminster (a frequent charge) should realise that, unlike the case in other constitutions, there has never been the 'conspiracy of silence' about the existence of parties:[69] on the contrary, the very architecture of the House of Commons speaks volumes about the place of party allegiance in the parliamentary process. The remarks on Germany, France and Italy show what the dangers are when party confrontations disappear, whether because of excessive consensus or because of excessive fragmentation between parties. Bagehot recognised that the party system in Westminster was the 'bone of its bone, breath of its breath',[70] emphasising that the function of parliament is to bring out differences of opinion into the open, offering parliament and public a real choice by so doing. Parliamentary discussions are not meant to reveal a general will which already exists and then to enshrine it in law, but instead to reflect the conflicts within society and to constitute opinion and judgement as a result of proposal and counter-proposal, on information and the asking of questions.

In comparison with the constitutions of other countries in Europe it is difficult in Britain to substantiate the charge of excessive domination of the executive over a legislature. Under Mrs Thatcher a major improvement in parliamentary control of the executive was introduced with the creation of the select committee system in 1979.[71] They, among other things, have put Westminster into that category of parliaments which can and do exercise a significant degree of influence over the formation of policy. In 1986 the Prime Minister listed 150 select committee policy recommendations accepted by the government that year.[72] Other academic studies have agreed that Westminster has increased its capacity for scrutiny and influence on policy over recent years, not decreased it.[73] Scrutiny of EC legislation is not perfect but it is far better than in all other Parliaments in Europe, except the Folketing in Denmark. The new Standing Committee procedure with the cross examination of Ministers is a preliminary step in the right direction but there is a great need for earlier involvement in the process. Where party discipline is concerned, it is clear that voting cohesion has decreased over the last decade as MPs on both sides feel able to vote more freely.[74] Moreover, Mrs Thatcher's government had suffered 120 defeats in the House of Lords by 1990.

The ability of individual members to introduce legislation hardly exists in France or Germany, despite protests from deputies there.[75] In France and Germany only representatives of parties are elected, not individuals, and this difference in constitutional theory makes individual action by politicians there far more difficult that it is in Westminster. Private Members' Bills not only preserve an important margin of policy initiative for backbench MPs, but Westminster's increasing role as a centre for interest lobbying also strengthens its function as the crucible of interest representation in political life.

Constituency activity, that cornerstone of the British constitution, has increased significantly. While in 1971 MPs spent an average of 11 hours a week on constituency duties, the average in 1982 was 16 hours. Three-quarters of MPs receive between 20 and 50 letters a day, whereas in the 1960s they would have had this many in a week.[76] British voters are twice as likely to know the name of their MP than their American counterparts. In 1978 75% of those who wrote to their MP considered they had 'good' or 'very good' replies.[77] In its legislative and scrutiny activities, Westminster is one of the most active in Europe, sitting for far longer than most other assemblies.

Above all, Westminster enjoys a very high degree of support and interest among British voters, and it thus preserves the authority of the political system as a whole: 'The extent to which Parliament has served to maintain support for the political system constitutes one of the most fascinating aspects of the institution in the British political system'.[78] The 1985 Report on Social Attitudes found that the most highly valued method of taking personal action against an unjust law being considered was to write to the local MP and, although the importance of contacting the media for this purpose has increased, the 1986 report found 'a widespread and growing self confidence on the part of the electorate to try to bring influence to bear on Parliament'. The percentage of people who despise politicians or the political process is very low. Contrast this with the withering verdict delivered by the French on their political class and parliament.[79]

> Westminster scores well on most of the indicators suggested by Merzey for determining a more supported legislature. It has demonstrated impressive institutional continuity; it has not been the subject of serious attacks by the executive.[80]

Appendix 4 to the 17th Report of the House of Lords Select Committee on the European Community states that 'Parliament does not require to be consulted before or during negotiations on a treaty or before a text is initialled'. Surely a treaty vitally affecting the United Kingdom electorate's future democracy must be brought before Parliament before negotiations are concluded.

If the countries of the EC all give up national power and pass it to the European level, are they all giving up the same thing? It appears not.

5

A European Germany and a German Europe

It characterises the Germans that they never cease to ask the question, 'What is German?'

Friedrich Nietzsche, *Beyond Good and Evil*, 1885.

Is not the destiny of the German the universal destiny of man, in that he is the only one to undergo all the moments of other peoples in order in the end to present the highest and richest unity of which human nature is capable?

F.W.J. Schelling, letter to Weitz, 12 February 1849.

It belongs to German nature to present oneself as un-German: a tendency to cosmopolitanism, to undermine the sense of nationhood are inseparable from the essence of German nationality; the idea that one must lose one's Germanness as much as possible in order to find it, that any restriction to the purely German is felt to be barbaric.

Thomas Mann, *Reflections of an Unpolitical Man*, 1919.

Europe is our destiny.

Helmut Kohl, 1990.

The European Community is the creation of the foreign policy needs of France and Germany. Their post-war reconciliation lay at the heart of its foundations and the Franco-German axis is still its 'motor'.[1]

In Churchill's speech in Zurich in 1946 he laid down his ideas for a 'kind of United States of Europe': 'The first step in the re-creation of the European family must be a partnership between France and Germany. In this way France can recover the moral leadership of Europe.'[2]

He returned to this theme again in 1953, declaring: 'There is no hope for the safety and freedom of western Europe except by the laying aside for ever of the ancient feud between the Teuton and the Gaul. It is seven years since, at Zurich, I appealed to France to take Germany by the hand and lead her back into the European family.'[3]

French foreign policy has been preoccupied with Germany ever since. Despite his well known views on EC federalism, de Gaulle's first concern was with Germany, although, unlike his successors, he did not want to employ supranational structures to contain Germany. When he and Adenauer met for the first time, de Gaulle records, 'We discussed Europe at length. Adenauer agreed with me that there could be no question of submerging the identity of our two nations in a stateless institution.'[4] Some have even seen Mitterrand's current policy on Europe as the natural continuation of de Gaulle's, even though their views on the EC are so different.[5]

The Franco-German axis styles itself as the leading force in the Community and, while both countries make explicit reference to their special relationship in speeches in each other's countries, the primacy of this alliance is clearly played down in the other countries of the EC, not least because it negates the whole point of having a community. As Churchill said, 'if well and truly built, the structure of the United States of Europe will be such as to make the material strength of a single state less important'.[6] There are, however, occasional admissions of this policy in the British press.[7] It enables both countries to augment their own dominant positions within the Community while pretending to be acting for the sake of 'Europe'.

However, the Franco-German relationship, for all its sweetness and light in public, is a complicated relationship. The history of three German invasions in less than a century, together with the ambiguous record of the French under German occupation onwards, and the sudden, unexpected, role as one of the victorious powers, have left a mixed historical residue composed of fear, awe and mistrust. 'The Germans are a great people, a very great people', declared de Gaulle at Stalingrad. 'Let us never forget that they got this far. A great people, who perpetually tend towards war because they think of nothing but domination, capable of extraordinary efforts and extreme sacrifices in order to crush others'.[8] While the British press is usually circumspect in discussing the German question, there are frequent articles in the French press about the dangers of German domination.[9] It was evidently in this spirit of worry that President Mitterrand urged the French people to 'have confidence in themselves' as German unification came onto the agenda.[10]

It is difficult to exaggerate how many eggs the French have in the

EC-German basket. The relationship risked serious derailment over German unification, when Bonn failed to consult Paris before announcing its ten-point plan for unification only days after the dinner party summit at the Elysée Palace at which German unification had not been mentioned.[11] Nor were the Germans much amused by M. Mitterrand's initial coolness towards reunification[12] and his trip to Mr Gorbachev in Kiev in December 1989 to try to stop it. Mitterrand still seemed rattled in September 1990 at the summit which preceded unification in October.[13]

France has a persistent trade deficit with Germany and this is sometimes a bone of contention between the two countries.[14] Indeed, France even had a kind of mini-Ridley affair when the (then) Minister for European Affairs (now Prime Minister), Edith Cresson, resigned from Michel Rocard's government in October 1990 because she resented Germany's hostility to French investment in East Germany. In a report to the Conseil des Ministres (the Cabinet) she wrote, 'Our companies often encounter resistance from West German companies in gaining access to the best parts of this market',[15] adding later, 'I am very European, but it is quite unacceptable to build Europe on the basis of an imbalance with Germany'.[16] A long article in *Le Monde*, which bore a cartoon showing Mr Kohl getting up from a dinner table to join some friends, leaving Mr Mitterrand alone and rather forlorn, the commentator wrote: 'The "special relationship" between France and Germany is such that all foreign policy questions have an impact on it. It is the jewel of four decades of French and German diplomacy and the pillar of any future European architecture... However, it must be recognised that this relationship has been significantly affected by the unification episode'.[17]

Despite these upsets, it is clear from the joint Mitterrand and Kohl letters on European unification (in April and December 1990) that French policy will remain the same, only more so. 'There is no alternative to the Franco-German relationship', declare sources at the Elysée Palace.[18] Comments in several papers have presented this policy as akin to Pascal's wager, a kind of philosophical joke which the 17th-century philosopher Blaise Pascal used to prove the existence of God. When faced with the choice of believing or not believing, Pascal, a gambling man, reckoned that the consequences of not believing and being wrong (eternal damnation) were infinitely worse than believing and being wrong, so he chose to believe. So it is with France's belief in Germany's fidelity.[19]

The code word for locking Germany into the alliance with France is, of course, 'Europe', although it is far from clear that using the methods of the 1950s, strengthening the legal structure of the EC, can continue to serve their purpose, since the legal structure itself would inevitably be more and more influenced by Germany.[20] The French continue to believe it, however:

> The French see their dreams of European domination being shattered as the 'centre of Europe' shifts from Paris to Berlin. Many fear that France could be relegated to a secondary role. Hence the importance of anchoring Germany securely within Western Europe by speeding up European integration.[21]

This is a massive strategic mistake. The answer to the German Question lies primarily in Germany itself. To hand her the key to the legal structure of Europe within EMU (including the Central Bank) and EPU with a majority voting system gravitating around alliances dependent upon Germany simply hands her legitimate power on a plate.

The Germans regard the French approach with the occasional flash of dry humour. Chancellor Kohl once tartly remarked, 'When you talk to them [the French] about economics, they scowl, but as soon as you start talking about their nuclear capability, their faces light up.'[22] The real motives behind their view of 'Europe' are clear, however, when the Germans remind them (as Genscher occasionally does[23]) that Europe is bigger than the Franco-German relationship: the former foreign minister, Jean François-Poncet, called this 'a hypocritical way of trying to abandon the Europe of Jean Monnet'.[24]

However, the German attitude to Europe is something which is determined by a massive historical heritage, and it is only by investigating this that both the motives and dangers can be truly grasped. To understand the German question, one has to understand Germany.

As the emigré Hungarian humourist, George Mikes, remarked (in *How to be an Alien*), the English have no soul, they only have the understatement. For this reason, it jars oddly for an English ear to hear words like 'soul', 'destiny' and 'national psyche' being the common currency of political discourse in Germany. If it is true that Britain has lost an empire but not yet found a role, Germany is a country with an identity crisis par excellence. A glance at bibliographies on the German question, German national identity and German history reveals this huge lack of certainty: 'Our New German Megalomania',[25] 'The Delayed Nation: On the political temptations of the German mind',[26] 'What is the German's fatherland?',[27] 'The restless empire',[28] 'A Nation without a home',[29] 'Who are we? The German Question as a theme of our political culture'.[30] A recently published bibliography on the German question and national identity is thirty pages long.[31]

German political history is the primary source of this identity crisis.

Her fragmentation into little states, split between Protestantism and Catholicism, has been exacerbated by a split between those who wanted Western or Eastern orientation: the West, represented by the rationalism and domination of France, the liberalism and mercantilism of England, or the modernism of the United States, stood for the individual standing in a contractual relationship to society, nation-statehood and world political power; while the East, represented by Russia and Asia beyond implied culture, tradition, anti-modernism, barbarity, community and political romanticism. Germany's ever-shifting political forms throughout the 19th and 20th centuries, from Customs Union to Federation to Empire to Republic to Third Reich, and her prostration after the war, sliced in two by the East-West divide, confirm in stark reality the lines of the 19th-century poet Hölderlin: 'it may be a hard word, but yet I say it, for it is the truth: I can think of no people more divided than the Germans.'

The problem of German national identity has been intractable largely because there is simply no credible political model in German history for the Germans to follow. In addition, the German question and the European question are inseparable: 'the German question is at all times a European question too.'[32] Living, as they do, in the middle of the European house, the Germans can never afford to ignore the neighbours. Moreover, the relationship with the other countries of Europe (a 'German' special path versus a 'European' path; East versus West) is a crucial part of German national identity.

For long Germany had a political inferiority complex because of her failure, as Germans saw it, to develop into a nation-state along the lines of the countries of Western Europe. This led the Germans to emphasise their strengths in things other than politics, especially culture (during the first half of the 19th century) and industry (during the second half), using these to build the German nation. Apart from their undoubted strengths in these matters, the Germans have also been motivated by the belief that Germany's (and Europe's) disunity was an unnatural state which had not existed in the past. The clearest exposition of this is the poet Novalis's essay 'Christianity or Europe' (1799) which describes the Golden Age of European (and German) unity before the Reformation. Culture, religion, art, war, economics – these successively became the avenues by which Germany could escape from her status as a political pygmy.

> The French and the Russians own the land,
> To the British belongs the sea,
> But we possess in the air-empire of dreams
> An unquestioned hegemony.[33]

This desire to achieve unity along German lines often expressed itself in a distaste for the legalistic rationalism of the West (France, England). Instead, a highly romanticised view of Ancient Greek society became a powerful ideal: a society united in harmony by the bonds of religion and culture.

During the 19th century, German philosophy blossomed. German idealism was born out of a rejection of British empiricism: Immanuel Kant famously declared that it was David Hume who had woken him from his dogmatic slumbers. Its two main preoccupations are, first, that reality is (at least in part) determined by the perceiver and, second, that individual freedom must be seen in the context of metaphysical necessity. These two beliefs, not overtly of political relevance, are to exert a profound influence on political thought. The first allows political realities to be brought about by defining them in the mind first and then applying perception to reality; the second leads to the belief in supra-personal historical processes, Hegelian determinism and Marx. 150 years after Marx and John Bright argued over free trade and democracy, it is not difficult to see who was right.

Politics is thus not conceived of as 'a contrivance of human wisdom to provide for human wants' (Burke), nor as a matter of interests, conflicts and political goals, but instead as part of the struggle between good and evil. The romantic philosopher, Schleiermacher, spoke of national loyalty as a condition of admission to the kingdom of God. Above all, this kind of political romanticism fosters the view that future arrangements can be attained when conflict and dispute will no longer take place, having been replaced by eternal harmony. Kant, standing on the threshold between Enlightenment and Romanticism, sketched a plan for eternal world peace[34] while his romantic successor, Schelling, was one philosopher among many to call for a pan-European or worldwide federation to achieve this end.[35]

Germany's failure to achieve political greatness further encourages the view that she has a great future before her. As Nietzsche wrote, 'The Germans are a people of the day before yesterday and the day after tomorrow'.[36] Germany, like a happy wanderer, must go off in search of its fortune, shaking off parental tutelage and political adolescence. It can also give to the Germans a sense that they have a particular mission to fulfil in life.

The rise of German national consciousness is sometimes said to date from the philopher Fichte's Addresses to the German Nation, delivered under Napoleonic occupation in 1806. Like many other academic initiatives, it seems to have gone largely unnoticed at the time, and its historical importance has been perhaps exaggerated by those who live between the covers of books, yet it illustrates that in Germany freedom is considered primarily as freedom from an occupying power, from external political domination. German history is characterised by such external domination, as successive powers on the periphery of Europe (France, Russia, Turkey, Sweden and even the USA) are seen by the Germans to have exerted control over its centre, dividing and ruling. During the 19th and 20th centuries, this came to be known as the policy of the balance of power, and was principally associated with perfidious Albion. It has led on repeated occasions to a sense of being hemmed in, of which the doctrine of Lebensraum was the most extreme example. The freedom which is sought is thus the freedom to break out of this position and to assert her strength.

This sensation of being hemmed in in the middle of Europe was heightened by the foundation of the German Empire in 1871, although it was Bismarck's great achievement that he united his country in concert with the other nations of Europe. It required a man of his statesmanship to steer his country with the required sensitivity. His successors lacked this, and after his fall from power, confusion broke out as to what Germany's role should be. Whereas Bismarck had wanted constantly to reassure the other countries of Europe that Germany was satiated, and wanted to act as an honest broker between East and West (his banker, Bleichröder, tartly remarked that there is no such thing as an honest broker), Wilhelmine Germany decided to make a bid for power in competition with the other great powers, chiefly Britain. Being in the middle of Europe, Germany could not do this alone and she formed an alliance with Austria, enabling her to hide her hegemonial ambitions under the label 'Mitteleuropa' (Central Europe). She saw (Central) Europe as her natural area of hegemony, and its culture as contiguous with her own.

When the Weimar Republic was founded, the feeling that Germany had once again been suppressed by victorious external powers was very strong: the division of Prussia into East and West, the imposition of reparations (the economic effects of which Keynes so famously and misguidedly attacked) and the association of republicanism and parliamentarianism with defeat all fostered the the belief that Germany had been stabbed in the back. Hitler exploited this resentment with great success. The fragile democratic institutions of Weimar were not able to survive the sense of defeat, the recession and Hitler's onslaught, and within fifteen years he was elected Chancellor.

The Nazis were not nationalists, they were racialists. A Swede was as Aryan as a German. This, and the alliance with Italy and the countries of Eastern Europe (Romania, Hungary) enabled them to present themselves as pan-European, fighting the war for the sake of Europe and for the new European order against the peripheral or non-

European powers. In this sense they were internationalists, and are typical of the German unease with the nation state: 'German nationalism did not get a grip on a timely, feasible concept of the state. Instead, people either reached for the mediaeval Holy Roman Empire as a model, which had been constituted quite differently and which was, as a result, very misleading in a number of different ways, or, hardly less disastrously, for the murky concept of the *Volk*'.[37] There is a rich seam of 'Europeanism' running through fascist thought, as a quick perusal of Nazi newspapers or a glance at the memoirs of British fascists like Diana Mosley reveals.[38]

Hitler's opponents also claimed 'Europe' as their calling. Klaus Mann wrote, 'I try to give a name to my longing, to name my inheritance and my duty. Europa! These syllables are for me the quintessence of the Beautiful, the Worthy, they are an inspiration, a political confession of faith and a moral and spiritual claim'.[39] Thomas Mann famously called for 'a European Germany' in 1953. Like their opponents, these anti-Nazis had stressed Europe's cultural heritage (rather as Germany's 19th-century philosophers had stressed Germany's culture and its superiority over the French) and sought to use this as a political model. It was a vague enough concept for the left-liberals to unite around, and became a kind of surrogate nationalism.

It is customary to think of the defeat of Hitler as a 'Zero Hour' in German history, when everything started with a clean slate. In particular, the rapid ossification of the Soviet hardline position in the East and the Cold War division which resulted from this meant that clear decisions had to be taken. 'Europe' was hardly a realistic principle, and Adenauer's policy was decidedly pro-Atlantic and Western. This was not to the liking of the Social Democrats, who took a more nationalist position, placing national unification above Western allegiance in their order of priorities, and advocating a spurious 'third way' between East and West, a kind of German 'special path'. This tendency has persisted on the left and centre-left ever since. There was a violent row in the Bundestag, for instance, when the SPD leader, Kurt Schuhmacher, attacked Adenauer for cosying up to the enemy by calling him 'the Allies' Chancellor' in 1949.[40]

Adenauer recognised the peculiar difficulties which Germany's geographical position imposed upon her. 'The Federal Republic cannot exist without the support of other states. Germany's geographical position is particularly unfavourable. She lies in the middle of Europe and has no protected borders...Now more than ever we need the help of our friends'.[41] The most important friend was the United States: 'We Europeans must be clear about one thing: without the help and protection of the United States, Europe was powerless against the pressure of the Soviet Union'.[42] 'On no account must the impression be created, above all in the United States, that Germany is wavering between East and West'.[43]

Furthermore, Adenauer was prepared to put the question of national unity on the back burner as a result of his clear moral choice for the values of the West. This was his most vulnerable political decision. He even preferred not to put the question to the vote in 1952 after Stalin's offer of unification in exchange for neutrality for fear that the Germans might well be tempted by that option.[44] The debate about the missed opportunity has continued ever since. Adenauer knew that he risked facing a formidable opposition in the form of a coalition of the SPD, the FDB (the small liberal party) and the Party of Expellees. He thus presented his Western integration as being in the interest of eventual unification. 'Only when the West is strong will there be a real opportunity for peaceful negotiations with the aim of freeing not only the Soviet zone [i.e. East Germany] but also the whole of enslaved Eastern Europe behond the Iron Curtain.'[45] Despite the apparent decisiveness of Adenauer's foreign policy, therefore, some have argued that there lay a fundamental ambivalence at the bottom of it, symbolised by the choice of his home town, Bonn, as the new capital: it represented Western orientation all right but, at the same time, it was very obviously only a provisional arrangement.[46] After unification the capital officially became Berlin again, as Article 2 of the Unification Treaty stipulates; however, the Bundestag and German public opinion subsequently agonised for nine months before taking the decision, on 20 June 1991, to move the government back to Berlin. The debate, a minefield of symbolism, showed once again how vexed the question of German national identity is.

Adenauer's policy had another unfortunate side-effect. His rigorous moral choice against communism strengthened a sense of moral superiority among the Germans, who felt that they were holding the fort for the free world:

> The people which only a few years previously had committed brutal genocide and waged a terrible war of destruction suddenly found themselves in the role of the great advocate of justice, peace and the protection of the West from the communist danger. Looking eastwards, the feeling of being in every respect a superior people with a concomitant missionary task found the desired confirmation...The German question became the key to peace and security in Europe, and without its resolution no détente would be possible. The peoples of Europe would come together only when the Germans had found their national unity.[47]

Throughout all this period the SPD and FPD continued to argue for a less exclusively western orientation, dusting off the old chestnut about Germany's 'third way' which had been so disastrous in 1918. Karl George Pfleiderer (FDP) spoke of Germany's 'middle way' or as 'a centre of balance between East and West'.[48] When the Berlin Wall was built in 1961 and the first killings began, one might have expected these siren voices calling for a third way to fall silent. (A total of 79 people were killed during the 28 years of the wall's existence, the last in February 1989; there were regularly about two escape attempts a week.) Instead, the wall was used as a reason for seeking conciliation with the East and accepting it as a fait accompli. Willy Brandt tried to present his policy as the natural continuation of Adenauer's: he would reconcile Germany with the East in the same way as the old man had reconciled her with the West. The policy became known under the slogan 'Wandel durch Annäherung' (encouraging change through rapprochement) and it led to huge financial subsidies to one of the most brutal regimes in Europe, considerably increasing the standard of living in East Germany and thus legitimising the absurd claims of Honecker and Ulbricht to have created 'real existing socialism'.[49] The fact that old *Stasi* agents are still in positions of influence, doing well financially out of reunification, has led many East Germans to fear that things have not changed. Moreover recent racialist attacks are worsening and spreading to West Germany, as *The Times* reported on 7 October 1991. Nearly 3 million refugees have come to West Germany since 1984.

Ostpolitik is a rejection of Adenauer (whose grave was recently daubed with a swastika) in several important respects. The treaty defining relations between West and East Germany (1972)[50] represented a rejection of Adenauer on two key issues: first, it accepted the legitimacy and moral equivalence of East Germany, and secondly it saw accommodation with East Germany as the key to peace in Europe, whereas Adenauer's policy had been to turn his back on East Germany in the name of freedom and democracy.

Ostpolitik dates from 1969 and the 1970s saw a resurgence of anti-Americanism in Germany. Anti-Americanism has old roots in Germany, at least if one sees it as a continuation of the anti-liberal, anti-mercantilist sentiments of 'Englandhass' (dislike of England). Germany, incidentally, shares this characteristic with France, where anti-Americanism is an accepted totem among intellectuals and politicians alike.[51] The more it becomes clear that the United States is the only military superpower, the greater the possibility that the economic strengths of Germany in Europe (and Japan) will be developed as a complementary factor. The United States has every reason to take note of this.

There is also much latent anti-Americanism in the Soviet doctrine of the Common European Home, which is so popular in Germany. It was first enunciated by Leonid Brezhnev on his visit to Bonn in 1981 and then subsequently made famous by Gorbachev. Gorbachev writes,

> A serious threat is hovering over European culture. The threat emanates from an onslaught of 'mass culture' from across the Atlantic. Indeed, one can only wonder that a deep, profoundly intelligent and inherently human European culture is retreating to the background before the primitive revelry of violence and pornography and the flood of cheap feelings and low thoughts.[52]

If this is what the Common European Home stands for, so enthusiastically embraced by the Germans on the occasion of Gorbachev's visit to Bonn in June 1989, then it is difficult to think of a more decisive rejection of the values of the Atlantic alliance. It is certainly a long way from the crowds cheering at John F. Kennedy's 'Ich bin ein Berliner' speech in front of the Berlin Wall in 1962 to the communiqué issued after Honecker's visit to West Germany in 1987: 'both states agreed to respect the sovereignty and independence of each other in both domestic and foreign matters'.[53]

Part of the attraction for Gorbachev was, no doubt, that he was viewed as bringing peace. This touched a raw nerve in Germany, the romantic desire to escape from conflict. Sir Julian Bullard, a former British Ambassador to Bonn, has pointed out that 'some Germans argue, in a single confident jump, from the reduced military threat from the East to the possibility of a world without alliances or without nuclear weapons'.[54] Nor are the 'some Germans' just cranks: Peter Glotz, a leading member of the SDP, argued that 'practically all Germans are in agreement that military alliances have to be made superfluous ...Europe cannot allow itself to become the superpowers' football. The further the United States regards the Soviet Union as an enemy, the more Europe will have to go its own way'.[55] Our old friend, The Third Way, is alive and well and mingling happily with the centre-left of German politics. When Honecker visited the Federal Republic in 1987, Oskar Lafontaine declared, 'Both Helmut Schmidt in his day and Erich Honecker now see themselves as balancing between their own security interests and those of the respective superpower'.[56]The veteran foreign minister, Hans-Dietrich Genscher, has done nothing to allay this idea, bluntly denying the debt his country owes to the west by declaring, 'There is not a capitalist Germany and a communist Germany, there is only one German nation'[57]. During the run-up to the elections in 1990 the SPD candidate, Oskar Lafontaine, gave high priority to the withdrawal of NATO troops from German soil, and even the Christian Democratic government allowed doubts to creep in about the level of their commitment to NATO when they refused to modernise their short-range nuclear missiles in 1989.[58] This instinctive anti-Americanism was revealed most clearly during the Gulf War, in which the pretence that the Basic Law prevented them from sending troops was a mere figleaf for their initial failure to offer any political support to the American-led campaign (Genscher remained silent for a week after the fighting began, although he and Kohl tried to make amends later) and for their inexcusable prevarication about supporting Turkey in the event of an attack by Iraq.[59] This was in spite of the fact that, among the four victorious powers, the United States was the only one unequivocally and immediately to support German reunification. Gratitude never was a prime mover in politics.

Genscher's remarks about 'one German nation' may send shivers down some people's spines, but what is objectionable is not so much the reference to the German nation but the implied moral equivalence between East and West Germany. It is as if the German nation transcended the difference between capitalism and communism, between liberty and enslavement. Above all, the remark represents a rejection of Adenauer's explicit attachment of Germany's destiny to the Western path, reflecting a long-term trend in German policy making. For many years, policy-makers have referred to the need to 'overcome the division of Europe', as if the primary wrong were the division and not the domination of the East by Soviet Communism; as if the Americans were as much a part of the problem as the Russians, rather than its solution. This centre-left anti-western nationalism has characterised SPD and FDP thinking since the war.

The reason why it has been possible to maintain the semblance of continuity since Adenauer is that the soubriquet is still 'Europe'. Unfortunately, the use of this vague and undefinable term fits neatly into the all too German habit of using vague absolutes as political watchwords.

It is not widely realised that Germans of all political complexions have identified the fate of their country with that of Europe. This belief has only been strengthened in the post-war period when indeed the division of Europe and the division of Germany were in fact physically the same thing. The Berlin Wall both epitomised and was in fact the East-West divide. However, the theme of unifying Germany by means of unifying Europe is at least two hundred years old. Romantic poets such as Novalis and Arndt[60] gave expression to this idea and made it famous, but it dates at least from Leibniz's great political tract, *Caesarinus Furstenerius (De Supremum Principum Germaniae)* written in 1677 which called for the unification of Christendom and, thus, of Germany.[61] With her political and religious fragmentation and unclear frontiers, Germany shares many of Europe's characteristics and problems. Germany lies at the heart of Europe and thus epitomises it. Far from providing an escape from old German faults, an emphasis on 'Europe' is likely to reawaken them. There are several reasons for this.

Germany does once again lie at the heart of Europe. This can easily lead to a straightforward identification of Germany with Europe. It is all too easy for the Germans to accept the glib axiom that whatever is good for Germany is good for Europe, and the 'European' gloss may permit them to pursue their own interests while trying to convince others, and even perhaps convincing themselves, that they are doing this for Europe. As Bismarck said, 'I have always found the word 'Europe' on the lips of those who wanted something from other powers which they dared not demand in their own name'.[62] Genscher has straightforwardly said that a strong Germany is good for Europe.[63] This begs many questions. Germany's economic strength derives from the fact that she saturates the EC and Eastern Europe with her exports. If, as seems likely, she consolidates this position via the single market, while gaining de facto control of the single currency, one could well envisage a scenario in which a strong Germany was bad for Europe. If industries in other countries were weakened or depleted by German domination, and if the single currency removed the competitiveness of weaker economies while the Social Charter, with its minimum wage, insulated German workers from competitively low wages abroad, then one could well imagine economic decline and rising unemployment on the periphery of the EC financing the German stranglehold. Even if this did not happen, the idea that in the 'new Europe' envy, rancour and resentment can be abolished by a Europe directive is optimistic to say the least. As Hobbes observed, men are not like bees, 'Men are continually in competition for honour and dignity...and consequently there ariseth among men on that ground envy, hatred and finally war...'.[64] Who is to say that the poorer countries of Europe are to be happy with a dominant Germany just because it is said to be good for 'Europe'? Finally, if Germany did become the true economic locomotive of Europe, then she could demand support from Europe if her economic strength ever began to falter, thus exploiting her weakness in the same way as she will exploit her strength.

The reference to 'Europe' is thus evidence of the old German characteristic of being what Thomas Mann called 'unpolitical'. 'There is in the political thought of the Germans an old tradition which allows consciousness to escape from complicated political circumstances into the promise of the pure idea'.[65] This is described by another commentator as 'a despisal of the grey, day-to-day business of reconciling interests, a fear of the pragmatic soiling of ideals through political compromise, a distaste for cool reason, which threatens to corrupt the hot dictates of the heart, the primacy given to principle, the loyalty to fundamentals, to ruthless coherence instead of to balance, to compromise, which is always thought of as "lazy" and close to "horse-trading" if not "treachery".'[66] It is not difficult to see how 'Europe', with all the unnatural passion that this word evokes among so-called pro-Europeans, might itself become one such absolute.[67] Indeed, the author recalls at the EPP Conference he attended in the Reichstag in Berlin before the last European elections, a leading German politican advocating a federal Europe in vivid emotional terms: 'My heart rages with passion at the thought of a Single Government and a Single Parliament'.

The plan to construct a political union in Europe on the model of the German Federal Republic betrays just this kind of defective level of political maturity from which Germany has suffered so badly in the past. The German romantic desire to escape from conflict and to arrive back at a state of harmony and unity is one of the most important psychological motives behind European federalism, and it ignores the basic fact that politics is always messy, divided and unharmonious. If the Community is built on anything other than a recognition that people and nations often disagree and argue, then it will blow apart in time, or, worse, have to maintained by ever more centralised power.

A concomitant attitude, indeed maybe a cause of this, is the German tendency to distort reality. The German Idealist tradition was born out of the rejection of British empiricism and some political commentators have urged that the legacy of this can still be seen in the idea that 'the Germans have only really to desire change in order to achieve basic changes in their position, and that these changes would in consequence alter the European scene so radically as to produce the longed-for peace'.[68] This might sound far-fetched until one reads Mr Genscher's speeches. When addressing the problem of Germany's pre-eminent economic power, he either just says it is good for Europe or he says, 'I think our neighbours should overcome the tendency to think in terms of nation-states', while the same thought is expressed by one academic: 'in many ways, it no longer makes sense to talk about Germany as a distinct national unit'.[69] This is the same as saying that reality can be altered by perception, and that the problem will go away if we cease to think of Germany as a country. Elsewhere Genscher writes, 'Our actions, and *above all our thinking*, are of special significance for the future of our continent'.[70] An action does not become good simply because it is motivated by a good will, or by the right kind of 'thinking', at least not in international relations. Real concrete problems, such as the fact that Germany is the biggest trading nation in Europe, 50%

more populous than France or Britain, that she holds half of the Soviet Union's debt and has lent more money in government-guaranteed credit to Eastern Europe and the Soviet Union, cannot be made to disappear with words.

This leads on to the final point. Germany's historical power-base has always been Europe. Her previous bids for power have been made in the name of Europe[71] and her economic and foreign policies are primarily 'European'. Her political and geographical position in the centre of Europe gives the Germans a sense of special national responsibility for the future of the continent. Lying across the East-West divide, the Germans began to feel they had a special understanding of world peace, as well as that they had been singled out by the 'Great Powers' as Europe's potential war playground.[72] In ecology the Germans take it for granted that they are more ecology-minded than anyone else, and that they have a special sensitivity for this too.[73] One would not be so sensitive about a little natural arrogance in a powerful nation (a fault from which other powerful nations suffer as well) were it not for the disastrous effect of the German consciousness of having a 'mission' in the past. Genscher has referred to Germany's 'mission' to foster peace in Europe[74] and has said very frankly that, 'We Germans can be the architects of a united and indivisible Europe'.[75]

The reason why there is such a consensus about Europe in Germany is that everyone can unite around this vague concept. Indeed, the Preamble to the German Basic Law of 1949 includes a policy leading to a United States of Europe as one of the constitutional foreign policy goals of Germany. The danger is that in the minds of many it is a form of veiled anti-Americanism or a form of surrogate nationalism. It is already widely acknowledged that Germany has been able to augment her political weight, especially in European affairs, by pursuing her interests under the European banner.[76] If integration in the EC increases, so will Germany's weight within it, particularly within an inner concentric circle or club of six or eight of the kind emerging after the Dutch Presidency proposals in September 1991 – and which Germany would dominate. How could countries dependent upon her economically exercise any meaningful constraint? It is already clear that economic and monetary policy would be profoundly German in nature, but so would the 'common defence and foreign policy'. If a European Union of this kind were ever to be formed, it would either introduce new tensions and resentment when countries found their policies increasingly dependent on the most powerful country, and thereby lead to the break-up of the Community; or, if it did somehow succeed, the future union would in effect be a greater Germany, balancing uneasily between East and West, inheriting and perhaps magnifying the complexes and instabilities of post-Bismarckian Germany. Policy-making in Europe must take the long-term view. It was 40 years from the foundation of the German Empire to the outbreak of the First World War: would a 'united Europe' last that long, and what are its prospects? Britain wants to work together with Germany in a fair and balanced relationship, based on free trade, co-operation and democratic principles. She does not want of be forced into a legal structure dominated by her. Plans for a united Europe stray into the darkest political territory, and must be firmly rejected.

6

Federalism

The lion and the mouse cannot confederate.

Constantin Frantz.

'When I use a word', Humpty Dumpty said in a rather scornful tone, 'it means just what I choose it to mean – neither more nor less.'

'The question is', said Alice, 'whether you can make words mean so many different things.'

'The question is', said Humpty Dumpty, 'which is to be Master – that's all.'

Lewis Carroll, *Through the Looking-Glass*

The word 'federal' burst into the European debate in Britain just before the Luxembourg summit in June 1991. Its sudden arrival on the scene must have been embarrassing for those who have been trying to deny that federalism was on the agenda.[1] It was a foolish tactic on their part, especially since federalist thinking is so prominent in the European Parliament, Commission and a number of member states. Their flimsy ruse blown, British and continental federalists try the unconvincing tactic of denying that the French and Germans mean 'federal' when they use the word, saying it means something else in other languages.[2] Needless to say, this is nonsense. Ultimately, it does not matter that much whether the future arrangements of the EC are called federal, confederal, political union or whatever, except that labels may affect expectations and may accord spurious legitimacy to Community institutions.

'Federalism', like 'Europe', is an ideal political slogan: it can mean whatever one likes. It has been supported by people as diverse as the 19th-century anarchist Proudhon and the Founding Fathers of the United States. More importantly, constitutional experts have found considerable difficulty in distinguishing federal states from unitary ones.[3] 'The operational differences between federal and unitary states may not be as great as portrayed by the constitutional-legal classics on federalism'.[4] While most admit that it is difficult to draw hard and fast distinctions between constitutional types,[5] others have actively rejected the constitutional-legal classification of states into federal and unitary as ultimately futile.[6] For example, this definition of federalism seems reasonable enough: 'a federalised state is one in which the several units and their respective powers are constitutionally or otherwise legally united under the ultimate power of a central state or government'.[7] Yet it could apply as easily to Wandsworth Borough Council as to the Free State of Bavaria.

There is little evidence to support the claim that federal states are decentralised. Some federal states are so centralised that it is doubtful whether one should continue to refer to them as federal. This is the case of Austria, for instance, of which it has been said that 'banished to insignificant social roles, Austrian federalism has taken on something of a folklore quality'.[8] If one compares the ratio of central to regional/local expenditure in federal and unitary states, there is no evidence that federal states are necessarily more decentralised.[9] The much vaunted 'subsidiarity' principle has nothing to do with federalism as such and everything to do with Catholic social theory. The distinction between federal and unitary states has been called 'largely spurious'.[10]

Moreover, federal states, whether they are based on Christian Democratic 'subsidiarity' theories or on Anglo-Saxon separation of power theories, have been unable to resist the tendency to centralise, from which all states suffer. 'For the past several decades the majority of modern federations have shown a trend towards centralisation in connection with economic development and social problems'.[11] This much is clear when individual federal states are examined, as the German Christian Democratic tradition shows.

Of all the great canards quacking about in the European propaganda lake, none is more easily shot out of the water than the one about German federalists. One commentator has referred to the 'atavism' of pretending that Germany is a federation of states. Of course, it is no such thing. German federalism is merely a cloak thrown over the relatively strong regionalism which persists in Germany, and it was a system adopted by Germany, with the Allies' approval, after the war as a way of preventing a return of totalitarianism, which is why the Germans associate federalism with the opposite of centralised power. With the possible exception of the towns of Bremen and Hamburg and the 'Free State' of Bavaria, where strong regional loyalties are important, Germany is a thoroughly homogeneous nation-state (before the annexation of the five new Länder, at least). The concept of co-operative federalism is more a convenient myth for the gravy train of the Länder bureaucracies than anything to do with popular sentiment.[12] Elections to the Länder governments are treated much like by-elections in Britain, as a way of expressing a mid-term opinion of the Federal Government, rather than as a way of choosing a significantly different local or regional government. 'The federal arrangements of the German Basic Law have less to do with real federative forces than with the principle of the separation of powers itself, and they benefit party political groups, their ability to form alliances and the bureaucracy.'[13]

The much vaunted independence of the Länder is more a mirage than reality. The Basic Law divides legislation into 'exclusive' and 'concurrent'. In exclusive legislation the Länder have no rights except those explicitly granted by the Federation (Article 71). In concurrent legislation the Länder must agree, but they do this via the Bundesrat, the forty-member Council of Länder Ministers. In other words, the power to legislate and to tax lies overwhelmingly at the federal level, and individual Länder risk being outvoted. The Bundesrat is a federal organ passing laws and raising taxes centrally for the whole country (Article 106). The idea was mooted to make the Bundesrat more powerful when the constitution was being drawn up: it might have resembled its much more powerful namesake under Bismarck's truly federal constitution. However, this idea was rejected in favour of a more unitary solution. Not only is the Bundesrat's consent not required for all laws (Article 77(3)) but, in addition to its power to overrule the Bundesrat (Article 77(4)), the Bundestag has virtual carte blanche to extend its area of competence, in virtue of an article which is a perfect formulation of 'subsidiarity':

> in the field of concurrent legislation, the Länder shall have powers of legislation as long as, and to the extent that, the Federation does not exercise its right to legislate. The Federation shall have the right to legislate in these matters to the extent that a need for federal legislation exists because a matter cannot be effectively regulated by the legislation of the individual Länder (Article 72).

The criterion for deciding whether to extend these powers is if 'such responsibilities are important to safety as a whole' (Article 91a), or the 'maintenance of legal and economic unity' (Article 72.2.3). These prerogatives, together with the constitutional requirement to preserve a unity of living standards between the Länder have exerted a strong centralising influence. This is a long term-trend:

> The Federal Republic has become more unitary since 1949. Legislation has shifted more and more into the federal domain, which was not what the authors of the constitution intended. The Union has completely exhausted its competence in the area of so- called concurrent legislation, where the Länder also have a role to play, and indeed in some cases has exceeded its responsibilities. The legal authority of the Länder has been reduced to legal administrative authority by the federal administration. Defence and foreign policy, the necessity of employing the latest technology in areas such as transport, modern economic and co-operation policy and the associated taxation and planning requirements, above all defence and social policy... – all these things exercise an enormous centralising, unitary and equalising effect. These tasks are concentrated at the federal level, far more than was foreseen in 1949, and with them naturally expenditure, bureaucracy and political power.[14]

This trend has been massively reinforced with the spectacular rise in the federal budget (DM 200 billion or 8% of GNP[15]) for 1991, putting Germany deeply into deficit. It is ironic that the British government should have gone through so many contortions over local government tax, finally to arrive at a system whereby the bulk of tax is raised centrally and distributed to the local authorities, while such a system has been the norm in Germany for decades. It is very difficult to see how Germany is less centralised and it should be clear that the 'subsidiarity' principle is merely an allocation of competence, as in the hierarchy of a company, rather than a distribution of power.

Similar remarks are true of the United States, where there has been 'a massive and successive increase in the central power of government'.[16] Successive presidents have tried to reverse this trend, without success.[17] This is in spite of the lip service paid to the proud independence of the States. Their increasing problem is that more and more lesser functions are being devolved downwards but without the resources to provide them. Federalism in the United States is under a critical microscope. Even Switzerland, for many the model for a future federal Europe, has not been able to avoid this trend. In 1877 a book was published entitled *Switzerland's Development into a Unitary State*, so the trend is long term; yet in the last few decades the country has undergone large-scale centralisation.[18] Although the constitution of the Confederation contains detailed regulations on the powers of the federal government and on the content of federal policy, all this means is that whenever a centralising measure is proposed, they amend the constitution.[19]

Centralisation by itself is not the problem: despite what the federalists say, 'centralised' states such as Britain are perfectly capable of being sensitive to the needs of the regions. Not only does Scotland enjoy greater differences from England than Bavaria does from the rest of

Germany (in virtue of its legal system, Church and education system), its needs and those of Wales are dealt with by having Secretaries of State and Parliamentary Grand Committees. There are few equivalents anywhere in Europe (with the possible exception of the Finnish Swedes) of the widespread Welsh language provision in schools. What is objectionable is that when centralisation takes place within a federal framework , as it always does, the result is a complicated, opaque and unwieldy fudge. The polite term for this is 'interlocked federalism'.

It is clear from the American and German experiences that the classical 'layer cake' view of federalism, where federal, state and local responsibilities are defined, has sunk together into a kind of messy blancmange. 'Everything has become inter governmental (in the US). Although in the 19th century, the Federal Government was involved in a range of state and local functions, during the 20th century it has become far more difficult to differentiate national from state from local functions.'[20] In an attempt to devolve power, the government gives money to the state and local authorities: as a result, Congress, which ratifies the grants, is intimately involved in the distribution of the money, and thus in decision-making. Thus, 'Congress has come to dominate the national politics of federalism, and its members have gained that dominance by crawling inside the details of federal grant programmes and examining the effects of the distribution of federal money', instead of the states deciding it themselves.[21]

The result is red tape, unaccountability and constipated government.[22] From the top down, the segmentation of politics means that different people care about different parts of the federalist puzzle and cannot work out whom to blame. There is therefore massive judicial involvement in policy making,[23] yet little incentive for anyone to analyse and tackle the problems of the system as a whole, ensuring that accountability in such a system is impossible.[24] For the citizen with a need, whether it be welfare, housing assistance, job training or scores of other tasks the federal government has tackled through its grants it is often very difficult to decide just who is responsible for what. The fragmentation of politics has made it extraordinarily difficult to bring a co-ordinated attack on overall questions about the system. This is bad for decision making and bad for democracy.

Germany and Switzerland suffer from the same problems. Here, too, the division of competence between Länder or cantons and central government is often far from clear: instead joint decision-making is the rule. The result is an elaborate bargaining system. In Germany, as in America, the considerable involvement of federal grants in the financing of the Länder, together with the fact that it is the Union which decides the bulk of taxes, allow for deep central influence on Länder policy making. This is very clear from the results of the monetary union with East Germany[25] and the subsequent massive mopping up operation in which the central government is engaging. In order to administer this vast labyrinth of bargaining, there are some 200 committees which participate in the planning, implementation and execution of joint programmes and investment activities. The composition and powers of these committees vary greatly, but the institutional complexity of interlocked federalism renders the decision-making process opaque and bureaucratic. This lack of clear-cut fiscal responsibility encourages overspending and obscures accountability. In Canada, where the debt exceeds $380 billion (56% of GDP), out of 465 federal and provincial programmes, 60% are duplicated at federal and provincial level.[26]

These matters of a more technical constitutional nature are perhaps not immediately obvious to the man in the street, nor even to politicians; yet it is incredible that there should still be people advocating federalism for the EC given the abysmal record of other multinational federations. Canada, Belgium, India, Yugoslavia, the Soviet Union: wherever there are distinct geographically concentrated nations within a federation, the result is invariably disastrous. By contrast, the only federations which hold together are the ones which are culturally homogeneous, or which are marked by a unifying national-cultural ethic, such as Australia or the United States. The United States manages by and large to unite its culturally and ethnically diverse population with the American dream, and this is still a very strong factor, but this is under increasing strain as the Hispanics grow in numbers and as the ethnic minorities grow in influence. Over 50 per cent of the population of many US cities are now ethnic 'majorities' – the whites having left for the outer suburban areas. The government remains overwhelmingly white Anglo-Saxon, as is the political culture. Switzerland is 75% German and of the seven members of the governing National Executive (a kind of Cabinet with a rotating Presidency), five are always German, while only two are French or Italian. This imperative explains the attempt at nation building in the EC: the Brussels Berlaymont is now full of stickers saying, 'Europe – my country' and uniform passports are being imposed.

Take Canada for instance. Two profoundly different national political ethics dominate. In English speaking-Canada, the prevailing political culture is liberal Tory, whereas until recently Quebec was rural and very Catholic. (As Chapter Four shows, the differences within the EC are just as great, if not greater.) However, this is not the only reason. Apart from the argument that there is simply too much government (eleven state parliaments and governments, a bi-cameral federal parliament and a federal cabinet with 39 ministers, all for a country with less than half the population of Britain (26 million)), it seems clear that the policy of bilingualism has rendered the government opaque and bureaucratic. Deep divisions in the democratic institutions of a country favour an accretion of power to the civil service. (This was the experience of France in the IIIrd and IVth Republics.) It is thus the public elite which mediates across the country's divisions inventing policies which are of advantage to iself and its clients. Joe Clark, the former Prime Minister, once confessed that, faced with the choice of learning of economics or learning French, he chose the latter in order to get on in politics. The federal civil service is the only part of Canadian society which remotely approaches the bilingual and bicultural ideal: this isolates it from real life in Canada and gives it the tendency, like the Prussian army, to believe that it is the sole repository of national values. In addition, Canada's failure to develop a two-party system has inflicted a chronic volatility and instability on the country's political life. The burden of proof lies with the EC federalists to show why the EC would not become like twelve Quebecs, as the author put it to Jacques Delors at a private meeting in Rome in November 1990. For that matter, they might like to show why it will not become like Belgium, where nationalist hatred between Flemings and Walloons has nearly destroyed the country.

The notion of hegemony is crucial. 'The hegemony of a single member state is not incompatible with a genuine confederation'.[27] The violence in Belgium, India, Yugoslavia and the problems in Canada have all resulted from fear of domination by one group within the federation (Walloons, Hindus, Serbs, English speaking Canadians, respectively). Nor should the American example be forgotten. 'Slavery was not the real cause [of the Civil War]. That was the assumption on the part of the Federal Authorities that the people of the several states were...citizens of the US and owed allegiance to the Federal Government as the absolute sovereign power over the whole country, consolidated into one Nation'.[28] Most non-Americans do not realise how large the Civil War looms in the American consciousness, and until recently (before Carter and Reagan) in the South 'federal government was regarded essentially as a northern outfit attempting to foist liberal urban values on the stately old agrarian Confederacy'.[29] It was John Bright, the Free-trader and democrat, who was Abraham Lincoln's strongest supporter in the British Parliament during the Civil War.

Holland's position within the United Province of the Netherlands is another example[30] but this never became violent. The most striking example of a state using a federation to augment and consolidate its power is perhaps the position of Prussia within the Zollverein (Customs

Union), the North German Federation and finally the German Empire. It is worth examining the history of German unification to see historical parallels with plans for the EC.

Prussia's hegemony in Germany throughout the 19th century is undoubted. The great historian, Heinrich von Treitschke, described the Empire as a 'Prussian-German unitary state' and this view persists.[31] While Treitschke demonstrates how economic union in the Zollverein finally led to German unity under Prussian hegemony, it is not clear that there was necessarily any kind of secret agenda from the outset, rather, the natural pre-eminence of Prussia combined with other historial events beyond her control.[32] Moreover, it should be borne in mind that the process by which this hegemony was established took nearly forty years, from the foundation of the Zollverein in 1834 to the Empire in 1871. When thinking about the future of the European Community, it is essential to take a long term view.

The roots of German economic unification lie as far back as 1818, when Prussia unified her own tariff system. Taxes were raised internally, on roads, bridges and in towns, as there were many enclaves within Prussia and other states belonging to other crowns or princes. As Prussia was divided between East and West, with other states in between, this had a knock-on effect and Hessen, which was sandwiched between the two, adopted the Prussian customs code in 1828. In the same year Bavaria and Wurttemberg concluded a customs agreement and a Central German Customs Union was formed in response, rather as EFTA was formed in response to the EEC. These various unions were all within the territory of the German Federation (Deutscher Bund) set up at the Congress of Vienna. This unilateral action by Prussia was opposed by the other hegemonial power within the Deutscher Bund, Austria; yet it is clear that there were those in Prussia who perceived the political prizes to be gained from taking the lead in economic union. The Prussian Finance Minister, von Motz, explained to the King in 1829 that he saw the economic union of Germany as the prelude to its political unification 'under the protection of Prussia'.[33] She knew that she could put economic pressure on her neighbours to build up a bloc of states aligned to herself.

This was the reasoning which lay behind the foundation of the Zollverein in 1834. The Zollverein is historically unique because previous unions of states had been military, not economic.[34] The economist Friedrich List (1789-1846) developed these ideas to the full. He saw the state not merely as a division but as a combination of labour, an economic community or union every bit as real as the household or firm, and far more powerful. The crucial market for a state was its internal market for he saw free trade within a state as the way to combine the state into one productive role.[35] Among other things, he stressed the role of the railways in unifying the country, advocating state responsibility for these, and state protection for nascent industries from the tyranny of English free trade. It is curious how often railways are used as metaphors in the modern European debate. His view became almost a national orthodoxy and Ludwig August Rochau, who is famous for having invented the word 'Realpolitik', once declared that German unity was purely a matter of commerce ('eine reine Geschaftssache').[36] Above all, List realised the connection with economic power and political influence over other countries. He saw that the application of machine power to manufacture had enormously increased the capacity of one state to capture completely the internal market for manufactured goods in another state. 'By this means, the peaceful penetration of foreign markets, a state that possessed all the outward political attributes of independence and power might nevertheless be robbed of the internal, material, politico-economic bases of such independence and power.'[37] The purpose of economic confederation between states was not, therefore, to liberalise trade but to transform trade between states into an internal market. Thus could economic statehood be achieved for the economic union.[38] These theories enabled Prussia to present herself as the motor of German unification, a metaphor which connotes both power and a leading role. This was consolidated by the desire of smaller states to make the best of their inevitable inferiority by gaining a place at the top table through federation, and by the gradual decline of Austria as the only credible rival for hegemony in Central Europe.

None the less, Prussian policy makers must have realised what was to their benefit and what was not. Others certainly did: Metternich remarked, 'in the great Confederation, there is arising a smaller union, a status in statu in the full sense of the term, which will only too soon accustom itself to achieve its own ends by its own machinery...and will only pay attention to the objects and machinery of the Confederation insofar as they are compatible with the former'.[39] Other factors included the fact that the liberal-nationalist unification movement looked to Prussia as the natural leader of Germany: the Frankfurt Assembly offered the King of Prussia the imperial crown in 1849 but he rejected it, disliking their excessive parliamentary vision for the new Germany.

There is little doubt that she pushed for the creation of the Zollverein, imposing trade boycotts if states were unwilling to join. When the various treaties came up for review (the Zollverein was made up of over 200 agreements), Prussia would often threaten to withdraw if the terms did not suit her.[40] The economic realities meant that Prussia's weight was thus far greater than the constitutional arrangements suggested: the Zollverein was administered by a sort of Council of Ministers which met annually in one of the capitals, and it took decisions by unanimity. (The veto was not abolished until the foundation of the North German Federation in 1867.[41]) Moreover, Prussia was a net contributor to the Zollverein budget. Her benefits were therefore not so much economic as political: he who pays the piper calls the tune.[42]

The monetary arrangements of the Zollverein and its successors are of interest. Certainly, central banking was markedly different from our own day and monetary policy did not exist as an instrument of economic policy. However, a monetary union accompanied the Customs Union between the two halves of Prussia in 1818: when the Zollverein treaties were signed, one article (Article 14) committed the member states to discuss monetary union. This they did at an Intergovernmental Conference in 1837 when Hessen, defensive of its national sovereignty, suggested a parallel currency rather like the hard ecu. The scheme was eventually adopted in 1838, in preference to the Prussian plan to have the Prussion thaler used as the national currency for the whole of Germany, and at the same time the parities between the thaler and the South German florin were fixed. Thus a common Zollverein currency was used alongside the numerous other state currencies, which themselves circulated freely everywhere. This situation is reminiscent of the 'competing currencies' approach to EMU suggested by Nigel Lawson and then John Major, and ridiculed by Edward Heath as impossible. Final monetary union was not implemented until forty years later, after the foundation of the German Empire, when the Reichsmark was adopted in 1875.[43]

The Zollverein had been a subunit of the German Federation (which included Austria) and the North German Federation, founded after the defeat of Austria by Prussia at Königgrätz in 1866, was itself a subunit of the Zollverein, as it did not include the southern states (Bavaria, Württemberg). Flush from her victory over Austria, Prussia could easily have imposed the terms for the North German Federation on her partners, and indeed proposals were drawn up in 1866 for a union 'based on Prussian characteristics'. Instead of an Anschluss, however, Bismarck preferred to woo the other states to join a federation of their own accord. The constitution was remarkably like that of the European Community, with a Council of Ministers and a directly elected assembly. Prussia's pre-eminence was institutionalised in that the King of Prussia was ex-officio the chairman of the Bundesrat, but this was only as titular Head of State, not head of government: in all matters Bismarck was keen to stress the federal, decentralised aspects of the constitution, both to reassure the smaller states that they were not being swallowed up and also to convince Prussia that she was not losing sovereignty to the supranational authority either.

After five years, the initially reluctant southern states joined what then became the German Empire. Their agreement was bought with concessions to certain aspects of sovereignty about which they had strong feelings. (Bavaria was granted derogations on beer duties, for instance.) Bismarck still stressed the federal nature of the union, saying, 'The German Empire has its firm basis in the princes' loyalty to the federation (Bundestreue), in which its future also lies.'[44] Constitutionally this was largely true. The Empire resembled the North German Federation, except that the Imperial Chancellor was made accountable to the Reichstag: the rest of the Council of Ministers (Bundestag), which was the Cabinet, was not. This was in order to maintain the federal, not unitary, nature of the constitution. The Preamble to the constitution described the Empire as an 'eternal union' of princes and free towns. Bismarck soothed the anxieties of the smaller states with a Genscher-like formula about wanting a German Prussia and not a Prussian Germany although, of course, the latter was the result. In tax matters the Empire was indeed surprisingly decentralised, with taxes levied exclusively by the states until 1914 when imperial taxes were imposed for the first time. Even state passports continued to exist, although complete freedom of movement within the Empire eroded the importance of these. The Imperial Court was located outside Prussia, in Leipzig, as a gesture to Saxon sensibilities.

Moreover, Bismarck sold the idea of the Empire to the other states by saying that it would contain Prussia. He did everything in his power to assure them that Prussia was satiated.[45] The new Germany was to bind Prussia in and neutralise her:[46] it was to accord a security to the other states which they would otherwise have lacked. It was a typically hegemonial relationship if hegemony is described thus:

> I will use my strength to guarantee you and, in return, you must follow my lead with regard to other powers, and give me support and assistance when I call upon it... Hegemony is typically an unequal relationship established between a great power and one or more smaller powers which is nevertheless based on the juridical or formal equality of all the states concerned. It is not an empire. It is not based on 'ruler' and 'ruled' but on 'leadership' and 'followers'. It is held together not by command and obedience but by influence and what may be called allegiance...Great powers seek to guarantee their position by establishing a 'buffer' or 'barrier' of smaller powers friendly or aligned to themselves...but hegemony is not a one way relationship. Small powers seek also to come to terms with a particular great power either to guarantee themselves against the overwhelming strength of another great power or in order to prevent the great power in question from asserting its strength more

> directly and imperiously over them...Those states with the available resources, space and population at their disposal will sooner or later attempt to develop them to the point which enables them – to use the kind of phrase often employed publicly in this context – to 'play a part in world balance' or 'to take a seat in world councils'.[47]

It is difficult to avoid the comparison with present day Germany in relation to the other states of the EC and the quotation goes some way to explaining the motives for closer integration. The desire is to bind Germany into a new federal European order, while Genscher speaks of Germany 'assuming new responsibilities'.[48]

It can hardly be said that the German Empire contained Prussia. Over the forty years after its foundation, the federal Empire witnessed massive centralisation. The constitution contained federal and unitary elements and yet it was the centralising elements which won out in the end.[49] Indeed, Prussian hegemony fitted into precisely the gap between the two since, where centralisation took place, it was invariably convergence with Prussia, yet the commitment to remain centralised allowed her to defend her interests when she wanted to.

Immediately after the foundation of the Empire, there was a positive deluge of harmonisation and standardisation. The imperial authorities fully exploited and sometimes overstepped their constitutional powers: there were imperial laws for everything. One constitutionalist remarks, 'the codifications in this half century (1867-1918) exceed in scope, significance and long term effect any comparable period in German legislative history'.[50] Codification has the advantage over other kinds of state power that it generally lasts. There were imperial standards, industrial codes, legal directives, competition legislation, procedural codes, business and civil legislation, regulations for banking, foreign exchange, as well as imperial military and naval policy, foreign and colonial policy, tax and economic policy, the beginnings of interventionism and social policy: all this, to be sure, required more administration, greater power for the imperial bureaucracy and an overall accrual of power to the central organs of state.

In the overwhelming majority of cases this occurred with Prussia's blessing because the other states just adopted Prussian law. This was in spite of the fact that Prussia did not have a majority in the Federal Council: she could be outvoted.

> The right of veto in individual matters, the dependency of smaller states, Prussia's ability to exert pressure in issues such as transport, tax, defence, for instance: in short, her political weight ensured her superiority...Prussian ministers took the lead in the Federal Council, Prussian initiatives dominated in legislation. Prussian authorities partly

> took over the function of imperial authorities. Prussia's decision was de facto decisive for the most difficult political negotiations.[51]

It is essential to grasp the notion of 'political weight' to understand that, even within a federal constitution, the realities of power will predominate. States cannot be controlled with pieces of paper.

While she may have been forced to permit some seepage of sovereignty to imperial institutions on some issues, she was never prepared to give ground on things that really mattered as, in the same way, Germany is not prepared to give ground on monetary union. This was clearest in defence and transport policy: only Bavaria, Saxony and Württemberg did not formally transfer military sovereignty to the Prussian Imperial Ministry of War. Prussia also took de facto control of the entire railway network through the German Imperial Railways. It is in this sense that we can speak of Prussian hegemony: her economic strength, her size population and political weight inevitably resulted in putting a Prussian stamp on the new Germany. Her industrial codes, her laws, her ministries, her political and economic priorities, all these were in large measure adopted by the rest of Germany. The great German constitutionalist, Heinrich Triepel, writing in 1906, looked back on nearly forty years of developments within the German Empire and explained how the early guarantees that the Empire would remain decentralised were soon swept away in the flood of new laws, most of them imposed by Prussian ministries and conforming to Prussian practices. He also ventured a definition of hegemony, 'the totality of all laws and other arrangements by means of which the leading power of a union of states can give the community the desired direction and the stamp of its own spirit'.[52]

Are these observations relevant to the European Community? Unfortunately, there is a good deal of unhistorical thinking where the Community is concerned. One might expect politicians to talk fast and loose about 'a new European order', but it is depressing to see academics endorsing the view that the European Community is something so new and sui generis that the age old problems of the rivalry between peoples and states can be overcome through it.[53] In fact, it is precisely here, if nowhere else, that the EC resembles the German Empire: when the latter was being built many said that it was unique and sui generis. The national liberal politician, Johannes von Miquel, wrote that 'the suggested constitution could not be compared with the Swiss or American model', adding for good measure that 'great peoples do not copy'.[54] On the contrary, the federation or confederation of states, whether for the purpose of pursuing common goals, ensuring common defence from a foreign power or in order to come to terms with a powerful neighbour, is as old as the federation of the city states of ancient Greece.

The EC faces two big questions. The first is, how can the EC better operate together to pursue common interests? The second is, how can the predominance of Germany be contained? Even federalists accept that these are the issues.

This is not the place to dwell on the answer to the first question, although it is worth remarking that there are significant nuances of opinion between Britain, on the one hand, and France and Germany, on the other, concerning the relationship with the United States. Whereas Britain accepts the single market project within a framework of liberalised world trade in GATT, France and Germany have a more hostile attitude to the US, both politically and economically. 'American culture' is widely regarded as inferior to 'European culture', even as a threat. The French were delighted with the brave show of resistance put up at the disastrous GATT talks in December 1990.[55] It is clear from thinking in Brussels and Paris that their views on international trade owe more to Friedrich List than to Adam Smith, although it is always surprising that they bemoan their countries' so-called tutelage to the United States and at the same time attack the liberal economic policies which lie at the root of American power: why do they not realise that they should adopt economic liberalism as well? Instead, the Paris-Brussels axis firmly rejects it in the name of 'humanism'.[56]

It is in answering the second question that the historical parallel is illuminating. Can the Community resist the drift towards German-dominated centralisation? And is it not clearly in American interests to resist this?

Germans will argue that the problems are different since Germany is now democratic. 'The Germans have never been as democratic as they are now', says Herr Genscher.[57] Unfortunately, this is not the point. When Bismarck unified Germany he succeeded in doing so with the agreement of the other European powers, partly because of his own effective diplomacy and partly because he was able to reassure the British in particular that Germany's future path would be constitutional and parliamentary. It was because this was the case that the British were largely favourable to the foundation of the Empire.[58] The problem was that Bismarck did not last and his successors lacked his statesmanship and sensitivity to master the huge country he had created. The effect was akin to handing the keys of a fast car to a young and irresponsible driver. Future European arrangements cannot be built simply on the promise that the Germans will now be 'European', whatever that means, for the unification of that country creates problems which are more difficult to resolve. Who will be in charge of Germany in ten years' time? What effect will the withdrawal of troops from Germany have?

How will the vacuum be filled? What effect will the drive into Eastern Europe and into the USSR have? One very senior German official said recently to the author, 'Never forget, as Churchill said, the German people will be at your feet or at your throat'.

It is claimed that the 'principle of subsidiarity' will ensure that states retain a large measure of independence because federalism means decentralisation. This is one of the most dangerous falsehoods among the many which are advanced by the federalists. Subsidiarity is an old doctrine from German Catholic social philosophy[59] and has far more to do with this than with constitutional theory. Anglo-Saxon federal constitutions never mention 'subsidiarity'. The *Oxford English Dictionary* refers to the following gloss: 'a meaningless or even misleading phrase in English'. Indeed, it is ironic that it is being pressed into use for 'social market' theories when the original papal encyclical seems closer to Mrs Thatcher than Ludwig Erhard: 'that which the individual can achieve through personal initiative should not be the business of society'.

Sir Christopher Prout, the leader of the Conservative MEPs, claims that it means that the 'higher levels' of government (e.g. the EC) should be 'subsidiary' to the 'lower levels' (the national governments), a topsy-turvy explanation if ever there was one.[60] Elsewhere he has said, 'all that the concept of subsidiarity boils down to is an expression of the national interest of member states. In other words, if a majority of member states want to adopt a piece of legislation which has the effect of transferring sovereign powers from national governments to the European Community institutions, that is at one and the same time an expression of national interest.'[61] Whose national interest, he does not say. Whether one tries to illustrate subsidiarity by an upturned pyramid or a spiked helmet is irrelevant: Sir Christopher's definition makes it clear that, far from being a guarantee for decentralisation, 'subsidiarity' is a blank cheque for more and more power to be transferred to Community level, just as the principle's enshrinement in the German constitution has led to massive centralisation of power and expenditure in that country.

The normal definition, that tasks will be executed at Community level only if they cannot be satisfactorily dealt with at national level, begs the most important questions which can ever be asked in a democratic system: who decides? how? what for? The principle is a principle for the allocation of competence within a hierarchy. This no doubt explains why it is so popular in disciplined societies where the government is bureaucratic, like Germany with its proportional representation. It is anathema to the British liberal-parliamentary system, which is founded on debate and opposition. In this context the application by the Conservative MEPs in April 1991 to join the

European People's party (which is dominated by the German Christian Democrats) and its official endorsement have given rise to concern.

Subsidiarity betrays certain assumptions about politics which are not part of the British tradition. Indeed, Catholic theories of federalism are quite explicitly anti-liberal: a glance at the writings of one of the foremost theorists of federalism, Denis de Rougemont, shows the depth of this feeling. Having their roots in the sense of crisis which pervaded Europe in the 1930s, Rougemont's theories have been described as 'anti-parliamentary, anti-capitalist, anti-individualist, anti-liberal, anti-materialist'. It is difficult not to see the seeds of authoritarianism in this thinking: Rougemont says, 'C'est pour obéir que nous sommes libres': it is in order to be able to obey that we are free. 'Federalism is not meant to serve unlimited freedom, but rather the highest possible measure of freedom within a systematic order. Only through being exercised in a disciplined manner can freedom be preserved. Freedom within a federalist order becomes a question of duty.'[62] He rejects parliamentarianism and hates the nation-state, saying that this system merely takes into account people's interests but not their needs. Yet it is in this dangerous arrogance, that the politician can know a person's needs better than the person himself, that the seeds of bureaucratic authoritarianism lie. It is certainly not objectionable to say that personal freedom is sometimes limited: any society based on the rule of law does that. Liberalism is not anarchy. What is deeply objectionable is that the criterion for doing this should be the community rather than the dictates of justice. Federalism in its German form betrays a highly teleological view of politics, and its theorists arrogate to themselves assumptions and imperatives which are at best matters for the Church, but can never be pronounced on by politicians. Politics is not about the personal or spiritual development of individuals; it is about the never-ending process of trying to reconcile inevitable conflicts of interest. Politics is the art of the possible, not the science of the necessary.

Subsidiarity was designed to operate under forms of government exercising undivided power, and the pretensions and ambitions to exercise this power are already clear for all to see in the plans for European integration. Take monetary union for example. The Germans have made it clear time and again that 'in the field of monetary policy the principle of subsidiarity does not apply'.[63] Monetary policy cannot take account of the needs of different regions or countries and fiscal policy must not obstruct it.[64] Subsidiarity is also being dropped in other areas in favour of 'parallelism' – a more frank admission of the need and desire to centralise power:

> the Community's involvement in economic decision making should be based in a balance between subsidiarity and parallelism... Coherence within the economic union requires a decision making capacity such that the determination of policy at Community level avoids inefficient overlapping and contradictions in the various aspects of economic policy.[65]

The tendency to centralise power over time is frankly admitted by the Commission, albeit diplomatically: 'the list of policies which qualify on the grounds of being more efficiently discharged at Community level than at national level is likely to evolve gradually over time.'[66] Governments should not think that even this round of new demands from the Community will be the last, nor that the Eurocrats' appetite can be stilled with concessions here and there: on the contrary, the appetite for power grows with the feeding.

These integrationist trends are long term ones. For many years, people have been astonished at the 'revolting judicial behaviour'[67] of the European Court of Justice, whose determined promotion of European integration has surprised even the most ardent federalists. It has been accused of actually making policy itself, pronouncing on the basis of what it thinks the law should be rather than what the law is. This is contrary to the very fundamentals of the western concept of law.[68] There is not much hope for national authorities to defend their rights before such a court, especially if the principle and aims of closer integration are accepted in the Treaty Amendments, because in the past the Court has used similar apparent commitments to force the pace of integration.

Moreover, the harmonisation and industrial standardisation with which the German Empire was built is all too familiar a feature of the Commission's activism. This has not only created severe problems for the national parliaments, who are finding the huge quantity of legislation difficult to scrutinise,[69] it also respresents a seepage of power to Brussels, since the best way of attaining power is simply to grab it, whether or not you have a mandate. Where industrial standards are concerned, it is the Germans who take the lead. The German Institute for Standards (Deutsche Institut für Normung – DIN) has written more standards than any other country in the EC. DIN's role in determining European standards has been dominant, with DIN recently heading 40% of the EC standards committees, as many as France and Britain combined. Economic strength is the reason: unless you have German approval on a product, you are unlikely to be able to sell in Germany,[70] as the current hallmarking debate shows.

Not content with this, it is the German government which is demanding that further political power be transferred to the Community level, especially the European Parliament, where they will have the strongest presence, in virtue of the fact that Germany is now 50% more populous than any other European country. They have said that their acceptance of EMU will be conditional on this.[71] The French have generally been more reticent than the Germans on this point, aiming their efforts at economic and monetary union instead.

It is also clear that there are many in Bonn who believe that a tight union should be created at the centre of the EC, creating a two-speed Europe with a powerful core. Not only has the plan for a two-speed EMU been endorsed by Chancellor Kohl's Vice President of the Bundesbank, Dr Hans Tietmeyer,[72] but also geo-political plans for a Europe of 'concentric circles' based around an inner federal core of politically and economically integrated countries have been drawn up by Kohl's adviser, Michael Mertes.[73] The speculation aroused by the British Chancellor of the Exchequer's statements at the Ecofin meeting in September 1991 that there could be an inner core of eight countries served to emphasise the difficulties of reconciling such a proposal with a wider Europe and to draw attention to the two-speed concept. Pohl has also specifically mentioned that Austria could easily annex itself to this monetary union since it has pegged the schilling to the Deutschmark for years.[74] Italy might be considered an unlikely candidate for EMU because of its chronic budget deficit, which would have to be reformed first.[75]

Such an outcome, a 'two-speed Europe', would negate the very point of having a Community since it would concentrate economic and political power in a central core, leaving others on the periphery. Germany already pays a staggering 68% of the Community's income:[76] the system of 'concentric circles' would only increase her influence over the Community even more and if the club was reduced to eight she would unavoidably become dominant.

Accepting that a group of countries should proceed to a political or monetary union would be to accept the creation of a Greater European Superstate on the continent of Europe over which the non participants would have minimal control and which would be dominated by Germany.

7

A Hall of Mirrors: Maastricht and Beyond

> 'But you can't believe things which are impossible,' said Alice.
> 'Nonsense,' said the Queen of Hearts. 'You just haven't had enough practice. I often believe six different impossible things before breakfast.'
>
> Lewis Carroll, *Through the Looking Glass.*

The first formal and unequivocal statement of federal goals came from the Draft Treaty presented to the twelve by the Luxembourg Presidency in June 1991. It stated in its opening article: 'By this treaty, the High Contracting Parties establish among themselves a Union' (not an ever closer union). The Treaty went on to state: 'This Treaty marks a new stage in the process leading gradually to a union with a federal goal'. This caused a good deal of consternation and dismay in Westminster. The range and depth of the federalist objectives which were included in that draft treaty deserve to be highlighted, because even if the word 'federal' were to be omitted, the reality is clear. The trend towards a single government and single parliament was emphasised by the words, 'The union shall be served by a single institutional framework.' This was reaffirmed by the Dutch proposals of September 1991 driven by their Socialist European Minister. The draft even envisaged more centralisation ('a further strengthening of the federal character of the union') in 1996.

The Luxembourg treaty invoked the so-called 'principle' of subsidiarity, as discussed in Chapter Six. Nothing could be vaguer or more likely to lead to a greater increase in the powers and competences of the Community than wording of this kind. All major decisions could be construed as 'better achieved by the Community than by the member states acting separately'. Nothing would be a worse prescription for the future of the Community than for what are patently political matters to be left to the determination of the European Court, which is both unsuited and incapable of settling them.

For those who have been closely watching the developments in the current Intergovernmental Conferences of the European Community, the Dutch proposals of September 1991 confirmed their deepening concern.

These proposals were exclusively federal in design. They were rejected by an outcry from within Britain and by the British Prime Minister. They were soon repudiated by ten of the Member States, including Britain, but for different reasons, some tactical, some in principle and some (especially German) because the Dutch proposals did not go far enough. There were suggestions that the mistake made by the Dutch might derail the chances of an agreement at Maastricht followed by indications that the Dutch would 'trim' their draft Treaty, described by the *Independent* as having gone 'too far'.[1] Its rejection is less significant than its proposal. The drive for a federal Europe inexorably moves on. The electorates of Europe stand by as the squabbling continues.

The draft had proposed what was a departure from the Luxembourg proposals of June 1991 in that, amongst many other matters, it firstly would have placed foreign, security and judicial matters within the single framework of the European Community decision making process, together with, secondly, vastly greater powers for the European Parliament. The British position had been to press for intergovernmental co-operation on foreign, security and judicial matters (outside the European Community as such) and to emphasise the deepening of the democracy of the national parliaments of the Member States rather than of the European Parliament itself.

Underlying all this was the political influence of Germany. It was Germany which had pressed hardest for more powers to be granted to the European Parliament at the expense of the national parliaments as the price for monetary union on German terms. This simply reinforced the continuing determination by Germany to produce a conclusion in the Intergovernmental Conferences which would reinforce its preeminence in Europe, as previous chapters show. The European Parliament would be given not only a veto over matters involving majority voting in the Council of Ministers, including all commercial issues falling within the Single Market, but also a wide range of issues newly added into the competence of the Community. These, under the Dutch proposals, would have included the concept of subsidiarity, economic and monetary union, agricultural policy, social benefits, state aids, most social policy, structural funds, research, the environment, industrial policy, health and foreign trade policy (including GATT).

Foreign policy would have been liable to majority voting as well, despite the obvious failures of the European Community in this sphere in the Gulf and in Yugoslavia. A common defence policy was also included, implicit in the proposal for this by 1996 at the latest, a demand made again in October 1991. In a further rebuff to the British position, the underlying theme of a 'federal vocation', carrying forward the 'federal goal' of the Luxembourg draft Treaty, underpinned the Dutch proposals.

All this was the culmination of several months of 'separate' negotiations on political union and on economic and monetary union. Although there have been attempts to separate these in the public mind, they are inseparable. Control over monetary policy is political and a lack of control over it is undemocratic.

As to political issues: the Foreign Secretary had stated on 24 June 1991 that the aim at the Intergovernmental Conferences would be to conclude negotiations at Maastricht in December. He made it clear that at that point a judgement would be taken as to whether the draft treaty was acceptable or not. He stated that in the political Intergovernmental Conference there were three main objectives. Firstly, at present the twelve work together, both through the Treaty of Rome and through intergovernmental co-operation on issues such as foreign policy and terrorism. He made the point that the federalists want to channel all this co-operation through the institutions of the Community, whereas the British, the French and others want a model for the treaty which keeps these areas distinct. He explained that the British envisaged that the union, having at its apex the European Council consisting of heads of government, would have beneath it distinct pillars of co-operation, with the Treaty of Rome and intergovernmental pillars representing respectively foreign and security policy co-operation and actions against drugs and terrorism overseen by interior and justice ministers. He made the point that Community institutions and common rules are necessary for running common policies like those claimed for the single market, but that in areas such as foreign policy, co-operation should remain a matter for member governments accountable to the national parliaments. Secondly, on defence, the Foreign Secretary made it clear that, although Europe has an increasing role in respect of threats outside the NATO area, the movements towards building up a European defence identity must not weaken NATO or confront the Americans with a single European view. He stressed that NATO and America's presence in Europe remain fundamental to our security. He made the point that defence was not a suitable matter for the European Community, with Ireland being neutral and the likelihood of Austria and Sweden also becoming members of the Community by the mid-

1990s. He emphasised the importance of strengthening the Western European Union, making it a bridge between NATO and the twelve member states. He said that we had proposed setting up, through the Western European Union, a European reaction force but that a number of our partners within the member states had a strong emotional attachment to the idea of a common European defence policy associated with the European Community. Thirdly, he reaffirmed that it was essential to strengthen the rule of law within the Community and that in order to achieve a greater degree of enforcement and implementation of European rules, the European Court of Justice should be given the power to fine member states for failing to comply with court judgements. Referring to the June draft treaty in its aims to build upon the Single European Act by strengthening co-operation on foreign and security policy, he made the point that, as the Gulf conflict had shown, there was a considerable difference between the member states, but that there had been a considerable degree of united action in supporting the new democracies in central and eastern Europe in relation to the Baltic states and in promoting the Prime Minister's safe havens initiative. He emphasised the importance of strengthening the habit of co-operation and that this could be extended to cover security policy matters such as arms control and the CSCE and in relation to arms exports. However, he ruled out attempts to formulate foreign policy by majority voting which, as he pointed out, would have been disastrous in the Gulf and which were reinforced by the failed attempts to mediate in Yugoslavia.

On the question of increased competence for the European institutions, the Foreign Secretary made it clear that the significant shift sought by the June draft treaty to enlarge Community competence in areas covered by qualified majority voting was unacceptable. He emphasised the fact that, under the Single European Act, some majority voting had been introduced in order to ensure that the single market worked effectively, but that he was very critical of the case being proposed for further extensions of competence, for example in the social field. He made it clear that the Employment Secretary, Michael Howard, was not prepared to see Community action in the field of industrial relations and that Community legislation should not push up labour costs in such a way as to reduce the ability of business to compete in world markets.

Concerning the question of enhancing the role of the institutions of the Community, the Foreign Secretary made the point that work was being done to establish a more active role for national parliaments in considering Community legislation in line with the strong tradition of the Westminster and Danish parliaments. He stated that the British were not persuaded by the move for major changes in the institutional balance within the Community and ruled out the proposals for giving the European Parliament the right of co-decision over the Council of Ministers on legislative matters. He emphasised that the European Parliament should be given more teeth to ensure value for money and for scrutinising how the Commission spends taxpayers' money.

With respect to the issue of subsidiarity, he emphasised that the British view of subsidiarity was to have decisions taken at the lowest effective level of authority. In his view, there should be a clear test applied to ensure that the Community only does things which cannot be done well at a national level.

Both the Foreign Secretary and the Prime Minister have made clear that we in Britain reject the idea of a federal superstate. This represents a significant political difficulty, since there are other member states who support the idea.

Here there are two problems. First, how to persuade other member states not to insist on proposals which take us down the federal route and, second, how to avoid agreeing to wording which would be inconsistent with the wishes of the British parliament and electorate, while at the same time trying to reach an agreement. This is as difficult as trying to square a circle.

One suggestion has been that the Government would agree to amendments in December 1991, with the reservation that these would not be binding upon the United Kingdom unless and until they had been ratified and approved by the United Kingdom parliament. Of course, it has always been axiomatic that no treaty amendments can ever be operative unless and until parliament has approved them. In the debate in the House of Commons on 26 June 1991, the Foreign Secretary ruled out the question of a referendum (which needs a separate Act of Parliament) and, if, therefore, the question was to be deferred to a future parliament, the amendments agreed at Maastricht in December 1991 could become an issue at the next general election.

Both the Luxembourg Presidency and the Dutch Presidency propose one rather than two treaties. 'Both will also have to be integrated into the Treaty of Rome when finally agreed, if finally agreed.'[2] Within this single treaty, however, the Luxembourg draft proposes a system of 'pillars': for various areas of policy (security and foreign policy, domestic policy etc.).

However, although it is thought that the use of separate treaty pillars to deal with the new subjects is more in the direction of those who prefer the intergovernmental approach, it is difficult to imagine that this does not involve a significant transfer upward of relations between the individual member states. It hardly seems to matter how the method of dealing with the transfer of powers is affected if the net result is to move decision making in critical areas of policy away from the individual member states. At present it is proposed under the draft proposals that the European Council would 'define the principles of and general guidelines for the common foreign and security policy'. The Council of Ministers would then take responsibility for the conduct of policy within guidelines laid down by the European Council. The Council would have to act unanimously although it 'may stipulate that the detailed arrangements for carrying out joint action shall be adopted by qualified majority'. The British Government do not wish these matters to be dealt with by qualified majority voting. The Anglo-Italian Declaration of October 1991 is a movement towards 'the European defence identity' under WEU political control, but significantly is said to be 'autonomous, separate from the NATO structure'. With or without the pillars there is a very substantial degree of continuing integration and devolving of powers and competence away from Westminster and Whitehall and the British electorate to new institutions by formal treaty arrangements, whether described as co-operation or not. The Dutch Presidency declined the 'pillars' approach in favour of the single institutional framework. The Prime Minister has rejected this.

As to economic and monetary issues: on 30 May 1991 the Chancellor of the Exchequer made it clear that 'we cannot accept any changes to the Treaty of Rome which would bind us to move to a single currency or single monetary policy without a separate decision by the United Kingdom Government and Parliament'. He went on to stress the fact that 'we believe it both unnecessary and premature to ask this House to take binding decisions to move to a single currency'. He made the point that, 'Our rejection of the imposition of a single currency and a European central bank also stems from our view that monetary union should not be prescribed by the centre or by governments: rather it should be market based and market driven.' He stressed his scepticism about any of the advantages claimed for a single currency and stated that it would be easy to overstate the extent of the reductions in transaction costs, mirroring the same views which have been expressed by the then President of the Bundesbank, Karl-Otto Pohl. He made the point that a premature move to a single European currency would have severe consequences, with the heavy costs for the less prosperous regions of the European Community, who would become increasingly uncompetitive, with sharp rises in unemployment. It is also worth adding that this could easily be accompanied by severe civil disturbance in some parts of the Community. He added that this would lead either to a relaxation of monetary policy, in contradiction to the intentions of the system, or to pressure for a massive increase in Community expenditure to finance financial transfers to the poorer regions. He also rejected the idea put forward by Mr Schmidhuber, the German European Commissioner, of a European income tax. (Since then there has been a new proposal for an Energy Tax.) He pointed out the complete lack of convergence which currently exists within the European Community and that this placed severe inhibitions on the extent to which a single currency and a central bank would be workable. He went on to make the point that economic convergence between the member states was a long way off and said, 'Given our scepticism about stage three, we see no need to set up a central bank in stage two.' He also said that he regarded legally binding fiscal rules as unnecessary and undesirable. 'The draft treaty', he added, 'drawn up by the Luxembourg Presidency is a useful basis for discussion. But there are many areas where substantial amendment is required. We are a long way from an agreed treaty. Over the next six months the negotiations will become more intense. We intend to participate fully and constructively.' There was, therefore, a considerable difference of view between the British government and the proponents of the draft central bank statutes and the draft treaty on economic and monetary union. He made it quite clear that, 'Certainly the idea of a two-tier Community is one to be avoided.'

One crucial matter, therefore, is the proposed Central Bank whose draft Statutes if agreed would become Treaty law. One of the basic tasks to be carried out would be the formulation and implementation of the monetary policy of the Community, conducting foreign exchange operations, holding and managing the official foreign reserves of the individual countries and providing stability to the financial system. The Central Bank would be prevented from seeking or taking instructions from Community institutions, governments of member states or any other body. The proceedings of its meetings would be confidential. In the implementation of monetary policy the executive board of the bank would give necessary instructions to national central banks and the member states would be obliged to ensure that their national legislation, including the statutes of their national central banks, was compatible with the central bank statutes and the European Community Treaties. The governor of a national central bank would only be appointed after consultation with the Council of the Central Bank. The bankers themselves, of course, would be both unelected and unaccountable and could not be relieved of office except in exceptional circumstances: the only concession to democratic control is that the bank would have to draw up an annual report on its activities and monetary policy and present it to the European Council, the Council of the European Communities and the European Parliament. As the papers accompanying the draft statutes clearly stated, 'The single most important characteristic of monetary policy is that it is indivisible and that the responsibility for monetary policy cannot be shared out between autonomously acting bodies'. Nothing in the Dutch proposals of September 1991, which merely proposed a transitional European Monetary Institute, appear to displace these objectives as part of economic and monetary union for the mid-1990s.

Politicians are not as responsible for inflation as some would like the public to believe. It is a shared problem. Moreover, independent central banks cannot guarantee to solve monetary difficulties although they can help. On the other hand, if in a democracy unacceptable monetary policies are imposed on the voter, there will be severe trouble if there is no accountability – no one to blame – and no change. Opting out of such important political decisions (for they remain political decisions whoever takes them) would undermine democracy in Europe. Erich Fromm in his *Fear of Freedom* made the point. The statutes of the Bank as presently conceived would in any case hand over far too much power to the Executive Board. The question of who runs foreign exchange is equally important. But the real problem is that the loss of political control or the handing over of it to unelected bankers or to the control by other countries by majority voting is a withdrawal of political responsibility. This would be fatal to democratic decision taking.

Nearly all member states are, or were, agreed that they do not want a two-speed Europe, as the Chancellor of the Exchequer indicated on 30 May 1991. The notable exception is Germany, where plans for a Europe of concentric circles have been developed and from which German stands to gain the most influence over the Community. This would comprise a monetary union of some of the states of the EC at the centre, with non-members of the monetary union at the periphery. This is because Germany has for long insisted on the necessity of achieving economic convergence before a monetary union is contemplated, and on any realistic assesment, there is no prospect of such convergence for some time to come.

Most other states have taken the view that this negates the whole point of having a community of twelve. Despite this, Jacques Delors has offered his so-called 'compromise' under which all states would agree to join the monetary union in principle, but could in fact join at a later date, when they thought the time was right. There are many reasons why this must be rejected.

First, it would allow other member states to set the terms for monetary union. Britain would find herself under huge pressure to join the monetary union if she stayed out. Her relationship with the Community would become very precarious and difficult, after all the difficulties we have had to date. She would, in time, be forced to join on their terms. Second, it would represent an acceptance that the use of the veto had been abandoned. Third, it would mean an agreement with the principle of the central bank and centralised monetary and economic control, something which should be rejected on principle. Fourth, it would present the British parliament with having to accept a fait accompli. To say that a central bank cannot be 'imposed', or that its acceptance requires a separate decision of the British parliament, adds less than might seem, since all treaties have to be ratified by parliament anyway. Fifth, it would destroy the notion of a Community, since it would entrench the Franco-German axis within it, and create a strong core at the centre, dictating terms to the others. The twelve would no longer be moving together as one, which would be highly regrettable. It would place Britain in the position which the Heath White Paper (referred to below) specifically ruled out, and would represent the final, if symbolic, abandonment of the ability to use the veto. This would hand a huge victory to the federalists, who could centralise the Community even further, knowing that the member state veto was dead and buried. Sixth, as Jean Monnet always indicated, the Community needs Britain in. The French would not want to find that Britain was no longer an effective partner in the European Community and acting as a counterweight to Germany. This is one of Britain's strongest political cards.

The Chancellor of the Exchequer announced at Appledoorn on 22 September 1991 a five point plan for EMU while emphasising that the British position remained that of 'whether' rather than 'when' EMU would be agreed by the Government. Much of the discussion about these proposals dwelt upon the need for convergence between the economies of member states. The Dutch, as others beforehand, have preferred to sidestep the political and democratic issues inherent in EMU and the effect of this on national decision making and the role of the national parliaments in the areas of public expenditure, budgets and all that flows from these. It is certainly a cause for great satisfaction that the British Government has managed to bring inflation down to a level comparable to that in Germany, although this is due more to a high interest rate policy than to membership of the ERM. Indeed, this success is evidence of the value of independent economic management. By contrast, the economic downturn in Germany, temporary as it no doubt is, is despite the policy of the Bundesbank. It certainly could not be claimed that the improvement in the British position has anything to do with EMU. Indeed, the better our position becomes, the less EMU can be claimed to be needed in principle or at all.

It has been strongly insisted that a constructive British approach to EMU does not mean acceptance of it. The emergence of the Dutch proposals on political union which followed immediately after the Appledoorn meeting gave further cause for rejecting both, in line with the cogent arguments the Chancellor has given before for rejecting a single currency and a central bank – and more so.

'It is our position', he said, 'and if necessary it will be our position at Maastricht – that we cannot accept a commitment or the presumption of a commitment' to a single currency. This must remain the case, therefore, despite the details of the proposals and despite the apparent assumption implicit in a two-tier approach of having only eight member states with sufficient economic convergence. It was typical that much of the Euro commentary on the Dutch proposals kept on stressing that a two-speed Europe was emphatically not on the agenda, while clearly demonstrating that it was. It would be no improvement on this to argue that because all the member states have agreed to a two-tier arrangement, therefore the Community was acting together.

It was ironic to observe Germany's Finance Minister saying at Appledoorn that before deciding who would be admitted to the EMU (in 1997) and who would be excluded, 'There must be scope for political judgement.' The issue, it may be noted, was not whether there was a political dimension to EMU which required such judgement but merely who would be left out. Nothing could be more political. Indeed, it is becoming ever clearer that what is patently missing from all these negotiations is political and democratic convergence itself. Only the British seem to be interested in this. Most of the member states prefer not to raise it and it receives as little coverage as the German question itself when everyone knows that both are of critical importance.

Underneath the communiqués and pieces of paper lies the unspoken, undiscussed issue: the role of Germany. Many of the member states and potential applicants for membership, in private, will admit that whether for economic or political reasons and more likely both, they want to contain Germany above all else. Those now outside the Community want to come in to protect themselves and those smaller countries already in believe they will gain more influence by greater union and mitigate the power and influence of Germany at the same time. The Eastern European countries see the position in two ways. They have just escaped the centralisation and domination of the old USSR. They do not want this centralisation reimposed through a two-speed European Community which has already demonstrated dangerously exclusive protectionist policies and which would use them as a cheap labour zone and treat them as second class citizens. They do not want to be excluded from a German dominated European Community, nor included in one either. The solution lies in Germany itself – its attitudes, intentions and people. They can prove there is nothing to fear but not merely by claiming 'they wish to be submerged in a European identity', as it was put to the author. They would float on top.

If the Community with our acquiesence moved in principle to accept the underlying federalism in the Luxembourg draft, we would be breathing life into an embryonic but as yet unfulfilled strategic mistake made after the Second World War, that Germany would be contained within a supra-national structure. The idea was understandable then. Now, however, in the 1990s and since the reunification of Germany and the changes in Eastern Europe and the old USSR, the policy has become increasingly obsolete, increasingly counter productive and increasingly at odds with Schuman's observations in May 1950 about German industrial domination referred to in Chapter One. Up to and including the Single European Act in 1986 progress was being made. Germany is so far contained by her own will and by existing Community obligations. Now things are going into reverse.

What is happening (but is not yet 'history' nor 'inevitable necessity') is that, far from being voluntarily locked into a supranational legal structure designed to contain Germany, she is being handed the key to it. Moreover, as even the *Guardian* reported,[3] it is increasingly obvious Germany is becoming more assertive; whether over monetary union, political union or foreign affairs such as Yugoslavia.

The European Parliament with its multiplicity of languages, headphones and its recent history could not possibly cope with this situation, as Chapter Three shows. Indeed such a weak institution would merely reinforce the influence of the strongest and most influential power. Germany could thereby gain an overwhelming but legal influence, if not control, over the majority voting systems of the Bank, the Council of Ministers and now the Parliament.[4]

Another matter which is causing some concern is the extent to which member states, including Britain, have already committed themselves to agreeing to budgetary arrangements being supervised by the Europe Community.[5]

The European question is therefore even now the German question, as shown in Chapter Five, and the desire for EMU and political union remains the desire to contain Germany.

It has been clear that Germany will only accept EMU on her own terms and this was reaffirmed by German support for the Dutch proposals. Currently, her ardour for EMU seems cooler than it was when Kohl and Mitterrand demanded a timetable for EMU in April 1990. At that time, Germany needed French support for German reunification. Now, however, the Germans have made it clear that they do not want EMU until they have sorted out the costs of reunification according to their own requirements and timetable. 'France knows that there will be no monetary union without Germany so will do what Germany wants'.[6]

This alone should be enough to prove the point: Germany (and France) pressed for EMU when it suited Germany. Germany played a substantial role in the bank statutes, saying that she would only accept EMU on her own terms. Now, faced with a temporarily rising budget deficit, and no longer needing to reassure France about reunification, she is back-tracking. 'If others want to control us they would have to accept our conditions,' Hans Matthofer, the former Social Democrat Finance Minister in Bonn, has said. 'The Bundesbank would give up power over the Dmark only if there is a European central bank which is a clone of the Bundesbank. In the meantime, it would try to delay it.'[7] This shows political weight in operation, and it indicates Germany's intention effectively to run any future monetary union. The French idea that such a system can contain Germany is an illusion. By entrenching the banking arrangements to suit her own interests and by applying pressure on her economically dependent neighbours to vote with her, she could dominate the Community. Far better to allow Germany to compete with the other member states in free and fair trade, with shifting centres of gravity than to hand over the whole system to a legal order which she would dominate and which, once done, could never be reclaimed in the foreseeable future. Any attempt to unravel such a legal order in years to come would occur only after tensions had been so great as to make it break down: budget restrictions, leading to spending cuts, unemployment and civil disorder. The Community would disintegrate and Europe would face increasing instability.

From Germany's point of view, there are distinct disadvantages, since she will be the main paymaster. There are certainly political rewards to be reaped here in the form of political leverage and influence, but this would be the Germany we have all been told will not reappear. To be the paymaster, one would have to have very deep pockets to provide the regional funds to protect poorer regions of the EC, Eastern Europe and the old Soviet Union.

In assessing the future of the Community, two questions must be asked. First, what trends are already observable in the Community? Legal definition is important, but in the battle against federalism or any other form of undemocratic centralism, political will is decisive. What pressures are there for the centralisation of power behind the definition of words?

Second, if new treaties are signed on the present basis, what will be the precise commitments? An apparently small shift, such as from 'co-operate' to 'shall co-ordinate' can imply a huge transfer of power, especially if some central institution has the function of co-ordinating the economies of the member states.

For a country to be democratic, elections alone are not enough. It must have a well-functioning parliament which holds decision-makers to account, renders government transparent and scrutinises legislative proposals and other information. Without information, and without proper procedures for its scrutiny, there can be no free choice, and no democracy. In the European Community, it is unfortunately clear, not only that there is huge pressure for federalism, but also that it has been exerted largely through 'confusion' and by a lack of specific and accurate information for the public in simple enough language in the tabloids.

The biggest federalist 'confusion' is that we are already committed to economic, monetary and political union, and that it forms part of the obligations under which we placed ourselves on joining. Certainly, there have always been those who desired federalism, and others who spoke of it. Schuman in 1950 may have referred to a 'European federation' but this was certainly not explicit in any of the formal papers or treaties. Churchill referred to 'a kind of United States of Europe' in 1946, but emphatically rejected British membership of any European Federation in 1953.

When Britain entered the Community in 1972, Parliament voted on the basis of Mr Heath's White Paper, which despite advice to the contrary explicitly denied that the Community was a federation, or that it would become one:

> The Community is no federation of provinces or counties. It constitutes a community of great and established nations, each with its own personality and traditions. The practical working of the Community accordingly reflects the reality that sovereign governments are represented around the table. On a question where a government considers that vital national interests are involved, it is established that the decision should be unanimous. Like any other treaty, the Treaty of Rome commits its signatories to support agreed aims; but the commitment represents the voluntary undertaking of a sovereign state to observe policies which it has helped to form. There is no question of any erosion of essential national sovereignty...All the countries concerned recognise that an attempt to impose a majority view in a case where one or more members consider their vital interests to be at stake would imperil the very fabric of the Community.

The wording is crucial, especially the words 'where one or more members', since this is the critical issue today: for the European Community to function as a community, all twelve governments, with the expressed and informed decisions of their parliaments, must agree unanimously on the same principles and policies, especially when the future of their democracy is at stake.

Regrettably, there is ample evidence not only that Britain is being forced into a corner against her will, but that much of the pressure for federalism, in one form or another, is being exerted in strength and much of it behind closed doors.

A tendency to be 'economical with information' in explaining what is happening in the European Community has been endemic for some time. This has been particularly true of the negotiations on Economic and Monetary Union and Political Union. Despite repeated attempts to have a White Paper explaining government principles and policy on these negotiations put before Parliament, and even despite the Foreign Secretary's own suggestion during the leadership election that this should be done, nothing has happened. The author called for a White Paper in the last Business Questions fielded by the former Leader of the House (Sir Geoffrey Howe) and repeated his call after the Dutch proposals for the Intergovernmental Conferences in September 1991. Indeed, it has proved exceedingly difficult to obtain information or the text of successive Draft Treaties in reasonable time before debates or at all. Of course the government needs to maintain a negotiating position, but a lack of information of this kind generates misgivings about what is going on behind the scenes, especially when the negotiations have such a profound and dramatic implication for the British constitution, for its Westminster Parliament and above all for its voters. It is not credible to apply the normal prerogative in not consulting Parliament on these negotiations, simply because they raise such fundamental issues relating to Parliament itself and the British electorate.[8] It proved necessary for the author to exert maximum pressure on the Bank of England to have the Draft Statutes for the proposed Central Bank deposited in the Library of the House of Commons in December 1990. Even when British proposals for amendment of the European Treaties concerning economic and monetary union were made available in January 1991, these were not accompanied by the Draft Treaty on economic and monetary union which was then circulating among the member states. Similarly, such texts of the Draft Treaty as had been made available have only been provided to the Select Committee on European Legislation on a confidential basis and subject to private briefings. Indeed, the Draft Treaty which consolidated the thinking of the Intergovernmental Conferences in May 1991 was only made available to the House of Commons at 1.30 pm on 26 June, the very day on which the Draft Treaty itself was to be debated. Even Mrs Thatcher had no copy of this document beforehand, although it was, of course, available to Government Ministers well in advance. The situation has its farcical side from time to time, in that sometimes documents denied to the Library of the House of Commons are available through Agence Europe or the leaking collander of the Community institutions.

This approach has been followed for some time:

> The management of foreign policy does not help to clarify the issues at stake. The provision of information to parliament has declined over the past fifty years; diplomatic blue books no longer appear, official secrecy is more tightly applied. The Diplomatic Service has adjusted to the frequent gap between the domestic acceptability and international necessities by stressing the advantages of 'quiet diplomacy'. 'Much of our foreign policy is conducted on the sly,' one senior official recently admitted, 'for fear that it would raise hackles at home if people knew what we were pushing for ...the risks of such an approach are that the gap between domestic assumptions and international negotiations may become unbridgeable in a crisis.'[9]

This has been compounded by very misleading and expensive Europropaganda, heavily financed by the Commission and by Chancellor Kohl of Germany who has provided DM 1.5 million to Harvard, Georgetown and Berkeley Universities for 'German and European Studies'.[10] The Association for the Monetary Union of Europe published the results of a survey, which found that 'Among those who expressed their position clearly on the question of a single currency, 61% were favourable and 39% against.' However, on closer examination of the details of the survey, the 61% was really only 46%, the former figure having been concocted by ignoring the 25% who were indifferent or did not give an answer. On this method, the more 'don't knows' there are, the higher the spurious figures in favour. What answers would be given to such real questions as, 'Do you want the replacement of the pound by the ecu and the setting up of a European Central Bank so that economic and monetary decisions would no longer be taken by you and your elected representatives at Westminster but by unelected bankers?' or 'Do you want your defence and foreign policy decided by the majority vote of other countries?' They are not asked.

Indeed, it is only recently that the matter has come on to the political agenda. In the late 1970s and early 1980s, Europe was not a major subject for British political debate. It only began to create interest in 1985 following the Milan Summit and the impetus towards the Single Market, and especially after Mrs Thatcher's Bruges speech of September 1988. This set a new agenda for the European issue. Then came a series of Early Day Motions rejecting federalism, signed by up to 190 MPs (Ministers and PPSs not being able to sign by convention) and mostly tabled by the Friends of Bruges in the House of Commons. Greater discussion about the European question began to take place. The Euro-cognoscenti and the self-proclaimed saviours of the City and of British industry and commerce, in the form of small but well organised cabals of Euro-enthusiasts, purported to speak for the nation as a whole. A flood of Euro-propaganda heavily financed by European information funds and the European Commission has poured forth aimed at creating the assumption that the proposals for a Central Bank, the Delors Report of April 1989, and the federalist developments to accompany these were all inevitable and part of an automatic historical progression. No attempt to explain why this was so was ever made. Jacques Delors and the European Commission strained every nerve to get their arguments entrenched, but the scepticism of Mrs Thatcher and of the bulk of the British Parliament served to pour cold water on the federalist cause. The Prime Minister has rejected federalism.

None the less, it has been very difficult to know what the British people think about the proposals now before the Intergovernmental Conferences because they have not been asked and information has been very thin. This is despite the fact that no proposals have been of greater significance for Britain for several hundred years. The implications for Britain of the political union proposed in the current draft treaties are more significant than when James II abdicated in 1688 in favour of William and Mary. The transfer of sovereignty at that time and the subsequent Hanoverian succession was against the background of an infant parliament and precious little or no democracy. What is now proposed is the transfer of powers on a truly momentous scale with damaging implications for our democracy.[11]

German Monetary Union itself has proved some of the difficulties of the creation of a federal system with weaker partners and that this can create considerable instability.

Working in co-operation within Europe and with Germany is by far the best way to proceed, but not at any price. Price stability and currency stability are not exclusive ends in themselves. Both of these can be achieved without a loss of democracy but, once monetary decisions have been handed over to unelected unaccountable bankers, the mainspring of democratic decision making would be taken away and soon the whole of Europe would become robotic. Furthermore, there is no guarantee that such a system would work at all. Extending the powers of the European Parliament in line with German demands would be the final straw.

It is the ultimate irony that in the search for stability the solution which has been sought by the federalists is the one which is most likely to lead to the greatest instability in the long run, compounded by the prospect of up to 20 million refugees from Eastern Europe and the old USSR.

It is a matter of deep concern that the political engineers have taken such control over the system as to force others to react defensively to their proposals. The implications for democracy have not been thought through. The concept is generated more by ideology than by reality, and there is a dream-like quality about the manner in which it is being assembled. It smacks of political and economic defeatism. There is a remoteness from the everyday lives of people which is only just beginning to come home.

The Prime Minister has emphatically rejected a federal superstate in Europe, a merger of member states and a common European security, defence and foreign policy. There remain the gravitational pull of the draft treaties and the intentions of the federalists.

Determined German support for majority voting for a common European defence, security and foreign policy (foreshadowed by a Franco-German joint army corps of up to 100,000 men);[12] for community decisions over international relations;[13] for vastly increased powers for the European Parliament, including a veto over the Council of Ministers (in cases of majority voting) and increased German representation in that Parliament, are all indications of the bidding up of the stakes – if not at Maastricht then beyond.

A trade-off of monetary union for reduced German demands on these matters would be a delusion. Monetary union on German terms, even if only in a Treaty in principle, would concede the essentials of political union and would be an irreversible step towards a German-dominated Europe. Indeed one of Chancellor Kohl's closest advisors indicated in October 1991 that Germany is set on a completely federal Europe by the year 2000.

There is great momentum towards a federal system, or something which so closely approximates to one as to be indistinguishable. It is like a Hall of Mirrors. It will take an act of great political will to turn this drift around.

Notes

Chapter One: Britain for Europe

1. Speech in the House of Commons, 11 May 1953.
2. See *Voilà Luxembourg*, May 1991, p. 45
3. Ibid.

Chapter Two: Free Trade in the Global Village?

1. 'The Competitive Advantage of Nations', Prof. Michael Porter.
2. *The Times*, 15 October 1990.
3. 'The Hong Kong of Europe', BBC Radio 4, 15 September 1991.
4. 8 June 1991.
5. The Economist Intelligence Unit Quarterly Trends Report No 2 1991.
6. See 'La CEE deçoit l'Est' (The EEC is deceiving the East) in *Le Monde*, 12 September 1991; see also 'Poles quit EC talks in export limit row' by Boris Johnson in the *Daily Telegraph*, 10 September 1991 and 'With friends like these', leading article, *Financial Times*, 9 September 1991.
7. Prague, 5 July 1991.
8. Letter from author to Chairman of Select Committee on Trade and Industry, July 1991.
9. 'Who pays the price for the unlevel playing field?', Hines Communications Group Video, June 1991.
10. *Barriers to Takeovers in the European Community*, A Study by Coopers and Lybrand for the DTI, 3 vols, HMSO, London 1989.
11. 'Second Report into the Operation of the Single European Act', 14 March 1990 .
12. Peter Oborne, *Evening Standard*, 6 February 1991.
13. *Takeovers in the EC*, IOD, July 1991.
14. *Technical Standardisation in the European Community*, IOD, 1990.
15. *Daily Telegraph*, 5 December 1989.
16. *The Times*, 16 September 1991.
17. *Financial Times*, 26 August 1991.
18. *The Times*, 30 April 1991.
19. *Financial Times*, 8 August 1990.

20. See 'North American Free Trade Negotiations' in *Pacific Basin Economic Council International Bulletin*, July 10th, 1991.

21. See 'U.S. Agriculture: Hard Realities and New Opportunities' by Marvin R. Duncan in *Economic Review*, Federal Reserve Bank of Kansas City, February 1989.

Chapter Three: Sovereignty and EMU

1. The relevant parts of the Treaty of Rome, as amended by the SEA, are the Preamble; Title II 'Economic Policy', Chapter 1: 'Co-operation in Economic and Monetary Policy (Economic and Monetary Union)'; and Articles 102a and 105. See also Noel Malcolm, 'Lies, Damned Lies and Federasts' in *The Spectator*, 22 June 1991.

2. Karl-Otto Pöhl, former President of the Bundesbank, during a lecture at a conference entitled 'Britain and EMU' held at the London School of Economics, 9 November 1990.

3. See *Europe Relaunched* by Nicholas Colchester and David Buchan, Hutchinson, London 1990, p. 161.

4. See Chapter 1, 'The Internal Market' by Hans-Eckart Scharrer in *Federal Republic of Germany and EC Membership Evaluated*, ed. C.C. Schweitzer and D. Karsten, Pinter, London 1990; see also Georges Valance, *France-Allemagne: Le retour de Bismarck*, Paris, Flammarion, 1990, p. 281.

5. See *The Economist*, 'West Germany's brake on growth', 30 July 1988; Valance, op. cit., p. 280 on the deleterious effects of these high rates on the French economy; Colchester and Buchan, op. cit., p. 167.

6. Quoted by Colchester and Buchan, op. cit., p. 168. The memorandum followed the Amato report in 1988.

7. Many have made this point, including Boris Johnson, 'Ruling the Roost' in *The Spectator*, 8 June 1991.

8. See Colchester and Buchan, op. cit., p. 170 and *Financial Times*, 10 July 1989.

9. Interview with *Financial Times*, 24 October 1988.

10. Ian Davidson, 'Ambitious plans for political union', *Financial Times*, 27/28 October 1990.

11. 6/7 October 1990, just after Britain joined the EMS.

12. Colchester and Buchan, op. cit., p. 170.

13. See 'West German voice echoes attack on Delors', *Financial Times*, 15 August 1989. See also 'Pöhl differs from French on EMU', *FT* 2 August 1989.

14. 'M. Delors s'inquiète de l'hostilité persistante des Allemands a l'égard de l'écu' (Delors concerned at persistent German hostility to the ecu), *Le Monde*, 3 April 1990.

15. 'EC finance ministers hail change of tack by Chancellor (Major) over EMU', *Financial Times*, 2 April 1990.

16. *The European*, 11 May 1990.

17. 'Restricting the Bundesbank's room for manoeuvre...would be unacceptable to us and a German government which gave it up could not count on the support of the German general public, which reacts very sensitively on matters of price stability', Karl-Otto Pöhl, Lecture organised by *Le Monde*, 16 January 1990.

18. Subcommittee on European Affairs (Committee on Foreign Affairs), 26 June 1990.

19. 3 November 1990.

20. 'The chasm between the Berlaymont and the Bundesbank', *The Economist*, 22 September 1990.

21. 'Germany gets the monetary jitters' by David Marsh, *Financial Times*, 6 August 1991

22. Lambsdorff was indicted in 1983 by the Bundestag for his role in the Flick affair. Like his FDP colleague, Hans-Dietrich Genscher, he has a portrait of Bismarck in his office. See 'Lambsdorff writes off hard ecu idea as nonsense', *Financial Times*, 5 December 1990; Genscher also has a portrait of Stresemann, Foreign Minister under the Weimar Republic. See Georges Valance, *France-Allemagne: Le retour de Bismarck*, Paris, Flammarion, 1990, p. 95.

23. *FT*, 5 December 1990, op. cit.

24. See 'Hard ecu, harder problems, says Pöhl', by Wolfgang Münchau, *The Times*, 26 June 1990; 'Pöhl buries UK "hard ecu" plan' by Peter Torday and Colin Brown, lead story, *Independent*, 10 November 1990. Pöhl's position as negotiator is clear from these remarks, as well as from his discussions with Francis Maude, Financial Secretary to the Treasury, see 'Assailed on all fronts over the hard ecu', *Financial Times*, 19 November 1990.

25. See 'Pöhl says framework for European bank agreed', *Financial Times*, 9 November 1990; 'Pöhl calls for two-speed move to EMU', *The Times*, 10 November 1990. He had rejected this idea in September 1988, see *FT* 'Pöhl differs from French on EMU' 2 August 1989.

26. 'EMU train stopped in its tracks' by David Buchan, *Financial Times*, 8 April 1991. Buchan writes, 'What, then, is the coinage in which the Germans might be paid? The most specific item on the German wish list is more powers for the European parliament.'

27. 'Pöhl toughens stance over monetary union' by John Eisenhammer, *Independent*, 20 September 1990. For trade figures, see OECD Monthly Statistics of Foreign Trade, March 1990.

28. See *The Economist*, 29 June to 5 July 1991.

29. 'Kohl predicts German union by end of 1992', *Daily Telegraph*, 22 March 1990.

30. 'Don't back Bonn into a corner' by Lucy Kellaway, *Financial Times*, 7 November 1989.

31. See *The Times* and the *Independent*, reports on the Anglo-German summit in Cambridge, 31 March 1990.

32. 'Kohn will es wissen' (Kohl wants to know), *Frankfurter Allgemeine Zeitung*, 2 March 1991.

33. Colchester and Buchan give the following simulated instructions for making 'progress' in EC integration: 'Call an intergovernmental conference and dangle in front of it a carrot and a stick. The stick is the threat of a breakdown in the Community, the carrot is a pragmatic programme, with a deadline, that deals with a concrete need. Load a bit of federalist vision aboard as well...Sell the results to national parliaments saying that the whole confection is now untouchably fragile and the best deal that each country can expect to achieve' (p. 24). The Danish parliament rejected the Single European Act, and a national referendum was then held. However, the referendum was not on the merits of the Act, but on whether the Danes wanted to remain in the Community or not.

34. Colchester and Buchan, op. cit., p. 22.

35. Lecture to the Hamburg Institute of Economics, 6 May 1991.

36. At the signing of the Treaty of Noyen in 1516.

37. *A Guide to EMU* by Ben Patterson MEP, publ. Conservatives in the European Parliament, 1990.

38. Interview, 'Today' programme, 13 June 1991.

39. Lecture to the Mont Pelerin Society, Munich, 3 September 1990.

40. Colchester and Buchan, op. cit., p. 24.

41. 70% of Britain's trade deficit is with the Community, 30% of it with Germany alone.

42. *One Market, One Money*, European Commission, Directorate General of Economic and Financial Affairs, 13 August 1990.

43. *Economic and Monetary Union* published by the European Commission (Sec (90) 1659 final), Brussels, 21 August 1990.

44. Helmut Schlesinger, 'How to arrive at an Economic and Monetary Union' lecture to the Hamburg Institute of Economics, 6 May 1991: John Major, Testimony to the House of Commons Treasury Committee, HC 620, q.2.

45. Speech to MEPs in Strasbourg, quoted by Ben Patterson, op. cit., p. 12.

46. Lecture, Mont Pelerin Society, 3 September 1990. His successor, Schlesinger, repeated exactly the same worry in his Hamburg lecture, see note 44 above.

47. Draft Treaty on Economic and Monetary Union, Explanatory Memorandum, p. 3, published on 10 December 1990.

48. Martin Wolf, *Financial Times*, 12 December 1990, 'Champions enter lists for EMU'.

49. 'Mrs. Thatcher revealed as a German nationalist', *Independent*, 2 July 1990.

50 'Bonn: the Bundesbank loses some of its luster' by Klaus Engelen, *The International Economy*, June/July 1990, pp. 67-69.

51. See 'Monetary Policy' by Detlev Karsten in ed. Schweitzer & Karsten, op. cit. (see note 4 above), p. 44; Pöhl says, 'In my opinion it would have been better to gain a few years' experience with Stage One of EMU...before envisaging further institutional steps. But naturally I accept the decision of the Heads of State and Government and I understand the political motivation behind it.' See: 'Basic features of a European Monetary Order', lecture organised by *Le Monde*, 16 January 1990.

52. *International Currency Review*, October 1987, pp. 74 ff., emphases original.

53. Draft Statute of the European System of Central Banks and of the

European Central Bank, published 27 November 1990 by the Committee of Governors of Central Banks of the Member States of the European Community, Article 2.2.

54. 'A Major rebuff for Independent Bank', *Independent*, 4 April 1990.

55. Dr Rolan Vaubel, 'Monetary Union by Decree or by choice' in *A Citizen's Charter for European Monetary Union*, Bruges Group, December 1989. See also 'Private Money: The Path to Monetary Stability' by Kevin Dodd, *Hobart Paper* 112, Institute of Economic Affairs, November 1988, p. 60.

56. The former President of the Federal Reserve, who presided over a period of high inflation, Arthur Burns, explained his mistakes in the Per-Jacobsen Lecture, 30 September 1979, quoted by *Le Monde*, 2 October 1990.

57. Quotation from House of Lords Select Committee on the European Communities, 'Economic and Monetary Union and Political Union', Volume I, 30 October 1990, para. 83, p. 32.

58. See 'Le gouvernement économique pleinement démocratique de l'Europe' (The totally democratic economic government of Europe) by Paul Fabra, *Le Monde*, 11 December 1990.

59. Delors report, paragraph 21.

60. As Pöhl made explicitly clear in the lecture to the Mont Pelerin Society, 3 September 1990.

61. John Stevens MEP in testimony to the House of Lords Select Committee on the European Communities, op. cit., p. 21.

62. *International Currency Review*, October 1987, p. 78.

63. Ibid.

64. Draft Treaty on the Union, published by the Luxembourg Presidency, 18 June 1991.

65. The Germans made this demand at Ashford Castle, see *Le Monde*, 3 April 1990, p. 24. The Draft Treaty merely says that the penalties are 'possibly to be clarified in future discussion' (Article 104 A, note 1).

66. See for example, 'Une Banque Centrale pour l'Europe' (A Central Bank for Europe) by Pascal Salin, Institut Euro 92, 1990.

67. See *Le Fig-Eco* (Figaro Business Section), 21 November 1990.

68. See *Le Fig-Eco*, 29 January 1991, 'Un projet pour rallier Britanniques et Allemands'(A project to rally both the British and the Germans).

69. See *Le Monde*, 11 December 1990.

70. See *The Spectator*, 15 December 1990.

71. *International Affairs*, 66.4 (1990), pp. 675-695.

72. p. 678.

73. Select Committee Report on Economic and Monetary Union, etc., op. cit., p. 11, para. 14.

74. Other instances of use of the 'f......' word are: Michel Rocard, 'Europe's Federal Imperative', *Financial Times* interview, 24 October 1988; Gianni de Michelis, *The Independent*, 7 August 1990; Peter Schmidhuber, German Commissioner, interview with *Die Welt*, 27 April 1990... there are doubtless many more.

75. 'Economic and Monetary Union', European Commission, op. cit., Section 3.2 'Efficiency'.

76. 'Economic and Monetary Union', op. cit., Chapter 2, Section 2.1.

77. See 'Shades of sovereignty', *The Economist*, 15 December 1990; 'The Competing Borrowers Approach to EMU', *The Economist*, 7 July 1990; 'Champions enter lists for EMU', *Financial Times*, 12 December 1990.

78. 'Prospects for European Monetary Union' at the conference 'Britain and EMU', LSE, 9 November 1990.

79. Ibid.

80. Lecture to Mont Pelerin Society, op. cit., p. 11.

81. Draft statutes, 'Introductory Report on the Draft Statute of the European System of Central Banks and of the European Central Bank' published by the Committee of Governors of the Central Banks of the Member States of the European Economic Community, 27 November 1990.

82. The letter was published *Le Monde*, 9/10 December 1990.

83. Vernon Bogdanor, *Financial Times*, 28 November 1990.

84. Christopher Tugendhat, *Making Sense of Europe*, Viking, London 1986.

85. John Stevens MEP, interview on 'Today', Radio 4, Friday 28 June 1991.

86. Georges Valance, *France-Allemagne: Le retour de Bismarck*, Paris, Flammarion, 1990, p. 137.

87. *The Economist*, 9 March 1990.

88. 'Strained relations among West Germany's big banks', *The Economist*, 1 September 1990.

89. See Georges Valance, op. cit., pp. 142-143.

90. Klaus Engelen, *Annual Meeting News, Washington '90*, Sunday 23 September 1990.

91. Mark Almond, 'National Pacificism, Germany's New Temptation', Institute for European Defence and Strategic Studies, Study No. 12, 1991.

92. 'Should Germany cheer?' *The Economist*, 14 September 1991.

93. 'The New Superpowers' by Jeffrey T. Bergner, St. Martin's Press, New York, 1991, pp. 48 and 59.

Chapter Four: European Politics

1. See Boris Johnson, 'Shy allies who won't come forward', *Sunday Telegraph*, 4 November 1990 and Conor Cruise O'Brien, 'Thatcher calls their bluff', *The Times*, 30 April 1990.

2. See Sir Leon Brittan (a supporter of EMU), interview on 'Today', BBC Radio 4, 28 April 1990, and elsewhere; Conor Cruise O'Brien (an opponent), *The Times*, 30 April 1990, op. cit.

3. *Le Figaro*, 11 October 1990.

4. See Ian Davidson, 'Ambitious aims for political union, *Financial Times*, 27/28 October 1990: interview with Michel Rocard, 'Europe's Federal Imperative', *Financial Times*, 24 October 1988.

5. *Literaturnaya Gazeta*, Moscow, 'Integratsia ili suverenitet?' (Integration or Sovereignty?), Mihail Ozerov, 30 January 1991.

6. Mark Almond, 'The Guilty Men Fifty Years On', *The Spectator*, 3 March 1990.

7. William Wallace, 'Europe and the myth of Westminster: MEPs must spell out the truth about how our partners see us', *Independent*, 24 January 1990. Wallace is a former Deputy Director of the Royal Institute of International Affairs, Chatham House. See also the editorial 'EMU and Mrs. Thatcher', *Financial Times*, 2 November 1990.

8. See e.g. 'Die britische Fanfare: Englands Angst vor dem Untergang schurt den Nationalismus' (The British fanfare: English fears of decline shore up nationalism), *Frankfurter Allgemeine Zeitung*, 25 April 1990, by Gina Thomas.

9. First reported in *Independent on Sunday*, 15 July 1990 and subsequently roundly attacked in 'Staggering condescension', editorial, *Independent*, 16 July 1990. Quote from Timothy Garton Ash, *Independent*, 16 July 1990, 'What we really said about Germany'.

10. See 'La démocratie anglaise marche bien' (English democracy works well) by Gilbert Gantier, deputé for Paris, *Le Figaro*, 10 November 1990.

11. 'Full tilt at the mythical enemy', by Joe Rogaly, *Financial Times*, 2 November 1990.

12. See e.g. David Olson, *The Legislative Process: A Comparative Approach*, New York, 1980.

13. Norman St. John Stevas, Introduction to *The English Constitution* by Walter Bagehot, Collected Works of Bagehot, Volume 5, London, 1976, pp. 146-147.

14. S.E. Finer, *Comparative Government*, Penguin, 1970, pp. 281-295.

15. Karl Dietrich Bracher, 'Democracy' in *Europe Tomorrow*, ed. Richard Mayne, Fontana, 1972.

16. Hannah Arendt, *On Revolution*, Pelican, 1988, p. 260.

17. See Thomas Saalfeld, 'The West German Bundestag after 40 years' in *Western European Politics*, June 1990.

18. Michel Winock, 'Les français et la tentation anti-parlementaire' (the French and the anti-parliamentary temptation), *Histoire* (137) Octobre 1990. The word 'technocracy' is 'technoénarchie' which refers to the 'énarques', graduates of the toweringly prestigious École Nationale d'Administration (ENA) from which the political class in France is overwhelmingly recruited.

19. For British articles, see Ian Davidson, 'France's national identity crisis', *Financial Times*, 9 January 1991 or 'Mitterrand: the cure or the cause?' by Suzanne Lowry, *Sunday Telegraph*, 16 December 1990; for French articles, see the French press 1990-91 passim, e.g. 'Le mal français', *L'Évenement* 17-21 June 1991.

20. Title of an article by Maurice Allas, Nobel Economist, *Le Figaro*, 5 December 1990.

21. Pierre Bérégovoy, the Finance Minister, remarked on the 'pervasive role of money throughout the political system' on 'L'Heure de la Verité', Antenne 2 (French TV), 11 February 1991.

22. See John Frears, 'The French Parliament: Loyal Workhorse, Poor Watchdog' in *Western European Politics* July 1990.

23. See 'La forte abstention confirme la crise politique' (The high abstention rate confirms the political crisis), *Le Figaro*, 5 February 1991.

24. Ibid.

25. 'La démocratie en danger', *Le Monde*, 11 December 1990.

26. Michel Winock, 'Les français et la tentation anti- parlementaire', *Histoire* (137) October 1990, op. cit., p. 48.

27. See *Histoire* (137) October 1990, op. cit., separate interview.

28. Karl Bracher described in 1972 how 'the old parliamentary art of attaining political control and reaching decisions through penetrating speeches and discussions disappears and, indeed, it does so before the ideas of the public': see Karl Dietrich Bracher, 'Democracy' in *Europe Tomorrow*, ed. Richard Mayne, op. cit., p. 329.

29. Winock describes this in the article in *Histoire*, op. cit., pp. 44-45.

30. Alain-Gerard Slama, 'De l'antiparlementarisme à l'antipolitique', *Le Figaro*, 5 February 1991.

31. 'La nouvelle constitution' in *Revue française de science politique*, January 1959, p. 7.

32. 'Right and left rejected by Mitterrand' by Michael Field, *Daily Telegraph*, 11 May 1984.

33. Winock, *Histoire* (137) October 1990, op. cit.

34. Finer, *Comparative Government*, op. cit., p. 260.

35. Finer, *Comparative Government*, op. cit., p. 297. Donald Cameron Watt refers to 'that bureaucratic elitist conspiracy which led to the establishment, first, of the European Coal and Steel Community, and then of the European Common Market' in *How War Came*, Mandarin 1990, p. 132.

36. Speech at Bayeux 1946.

37. See Harvey Feigenbaum, 'Recent Evolution of the French Executive', *Governance*, Vol. 3 No. 3, July 1990, p. 264.

38. Published in 1964 when de Gaulle was President and when Mitterrand stood for election against him. Michel Rocard also stood for President in the same election: it is a feature of French political life that the same people have been around for decades.

39. See John Frears, 'The French Parliament: Loyal Workhouse, Poor Watchdog' in *Western European Politics*, special issue on 'Parliaments in Western Europe', July 1990, p. 32, op. cit.

40. John Frears, op. cit., p. 33.

41. For all these figures, see John Frears, op. cit., passim. See also S.E. Finer, *Comparative Government*, op. cit., p. 314.

42. See the interview in *Histoire* (137) October 1990, op. cit., p. 50.

43. See *Le Figaro*, 10 December 1990.

44. There is no equivalent of the 'Today' programme on the radio, only news bulletins with hardly any analysis or interviews. The only in-depth political programmes on television are the weekly 'Sept sur Sept' interview (Sundays) and the fortnightly 'L'heure de la Verité'.

45. See the report on a recent debate on Europe, 'L'indifférence des français a l'égard de la construction européenne préoccupe le gouvernement et les deputés' (The indifference of the French to the construction of Europe worries deputés) *Le Monde*, 21 June 1991; Jacques Delors was quoted on 'P.M.', Radio 4, 27 June 1991.

46. 'Today' programme, Radio 4, 15 December 1990.

47. Michael Binyon, 'Minnows' mixed feelings on European integration', *The Times*, 1 May 1990.

48. Albert du Roy, a Belgian commentator, in an interview with *Le Soir.* M. du Roy is a prominent political commentator in France as well. The interview was reported in 'Federal structure seen as a threat to the Belgian state' by Michael Binyon, *The Times*, 21 July 1989. For a full account of the constitutional problems facing Belgium, see 'L'evolution du régime parlementaire' by Philippe Levaux in *Pouvoirs* (54, 1990), a number devoted entirely to Belgium.

49. Observations at EPP Conference in Berlin (1989) attended by the author.

50. See *The Economist*, 17 June 1989 for an account of inefficient government. See 'Where did all the money go', *The Economist*, 2 February 1991 for an account of the spectacular scandal involving the apparent siphoning off of 50 trillion lire (£25 billion) from an earthquake disaster fund; or the report on 'Today' (Radio 4) on 11 January 1991, especially the claim by a prominent journalist from *Corriere della Sera* that the reason why the scandal was not being investigated was that there was 'a significant degree of complicity between the government, who would initiate the investigation, and those siphoning off the money'. The disco-dancing Foreign Minister, Gianni de Michelis, almost admits that Euro-government is the only hope for Italy in *Independent*, 7 August 1990.

51. See Paul Furlong, 'Parliament in Italian Politics', *Western European Politics*, July 1990, op. cit., p. 55.

52. See Yves Mény, 'Politique Comparée', Paris 1991, p. 217.

53. See Furlong, op. cit., p. 62; also House of Commons Background Paper No. 224, 'The Single European Market and the Italian Economy', p. 20.

54. See the very hostile book, *Agnelli and the Network of Italian Power* by Alan Friedman, London 1987.

55. Karl Loewenstein, *Verfassungslehre* (On the constitution), Tubingen 1959.

56. Ernst Fraenkel, *Deutschland und die westlichen Demokratien* (Germany and the Western Democracies), Stuttgart 1964.

57. Thomas Saalfeld, 'The West German Bundestag after 40 years' in *Western European Politics* July 1990, op. cit., p. 69.

58. 'Party patronage and politicization of the West German administrative elite' by Renate Mayntz and Hans-Ulrich Derlein in *Governance* , 2 October 1989, pp. 384-385.

59. Karl Bracher, 'Democracy' in ed. Mayne, op. cit., pp. 327-328.

60. See Saalfeld, op. cit., in WEP, October 1990, p. 80.

61. Policy is made after the elections in negotiations between the elected parties. This process can take many weeks, while the electorate waits to hear what it has voted for. See 'Die Koalitionsverhandlungen werden vor Weihnachten nicht beendet sein' (The coalition negotiations will not be finished before Christmas) in *Frankfurter Allgemeine Zeitung*, 11 December 1990.

62. Saalfeld, op. cit., p. 81.

63. Simon Bulmer and William Paterson, *The Federal Republic of Germany and the European Community*, London 1987, p. 168.

64. Bulmer and Paterson, p. 169.

65. Konrad Adam, 'Wenn der Staat zum Parteibesitz wird' (When the State becomes the property of the parties) in *Frankfurter Allgemeine Zeitung,* 2 March 1991.

66. See Irving Fetscher, 'Utopien, Illusionen, Hoffnungen: Plädoyer fur eine politische Kultur in Deutschland' (Utopias, Illusions, Hopes: a Plea for a Political Culture in Germany), Stuttgart 1990. The corruption in the Treuhandanstalt was reported on 'Today' (Radio 4), Friday 12 April 1991.

67. 'Im Vorhof des Elends' (In the Heart of Misery) by Roland Mischke, *Frankfurter Allgemeine Zeitung*, 2 March 1991.

68. Ernst Fraenkel, *Deutschland und die Westlichen Demokratien* (Germany and the Western Democracies), op. cit., p. 68.

69. Karl Loewenstein's phrase in *Political Power and the Governmental Process*, Chicago 1957.

70. Bagehot, *The English Constitution*, ed. Stevas, op. cit., Volume 5 of Collected Works, p. 295.

71. See Lord St. John of Fawsley, *The Times*, 11 February 1989.

72. Hansard House of Commons Vol. 98, cols. 396-446.

73. See P. Norton, 'Independence, Scrutiny and Rationalisation: A Decade of Change in the House of Commons' in *Teaching Politics*, Vol. 15 No. 1 (1986), pp. 69-98.

74. See John Schwartz, 'Exploring a new role in policy-making: the British House of Commons in the 1970s' in *American Political Science Review*, Vol. 74 No. 1 (1980), p. 37.

75. This was one of the demands of the twelve socialist *deputés* in their article 'La démocratie en danger' (Democracy in danger) in *Le Monde*, 11 December 1990.

76. C. Miller, *The Government Report*, London 1987.

77. B. Cain et al, 'The roots of legislator popularity in Great Britain and the United States', California Institute of Technology and Social Science Working Paper, October 1979, pp. 6-7. Ch4/vi.

78. Phillip Norton, 'Parliament in the UK: Balancing effectiveness and consent' in *Western European Politics*, July 1990, op. cit.

79. In *Le Figaro*, 5 December 1990, 'La forte abstention confirme la crise politique' (The high rate of abstention confirms the political crisis).

80. Phillip Norton, 'Parliament in the UK' in *WEP*, July 1990, op. cit., conclusion.

Chapter Five: A European Germany

1. For a good account of the founding of the Community, see the early chapters in Christopher Tugendhat's *Making Sense of Europe*, Viking, London 1986: or 'La naissance de la communauté européenne' in *Le Monde*, 6/7 May 1990.

2. *The Sinews of Peace*, Post-War Speeches by Winston Churchill, ed. Randolph S. Churchill, p. 201.

3. Speech, House of Commons, 11 May 1953.

4. Quoted by Tugendhat, op. cit.

5. *The Economist* made this point in a review of *A Demain, de Gaulle* by

Regis Debray and *Le Président* by Franz-Olivier Giesbert, 3 June 1990: 'M. Mitterrand's remaining years at the Elysée will be judged above all on his policy towards the new Europe. This is a Europe which de Gaulle, with extraordinary steadiness of vision, in part foresaw...It is clear that de Gaulle's main preoccupation was, as ever, Germany.'

6. Speech at Zurich University, 19 September 1946, in *Sinews of Peace*, op. cit.

7. In the French press it is explicit: 'Mm. Kohl et Mitterrand relancent l'Europe politique' (Messrs. Kohl and Mitterrand relaunch political Europe), *Le Monde*, 20 April 1990; 'Mm. Kohl et Mitterrand relancent en commun la dynamique européenne', *Le Monde*, 10 December 1990. In the British press see Helmut Schmidt and Valérie Giscard d'Éstaing in *The Times*, 14 February 1990 and the reply to it by William Cash, 'Grinding their own axis', *The Times*, 26 February 1990.

8. 'France-Allemagne: l'artisan de la reconciliation' by Ernst Weidenfeld, *Le Figaro*, 19 November 1990.

9. See especially the French press at the time of German unification, especially *Le Point*, 1 October 1990, 'Quelle Allemagne va naître?: l'inquiétude française' (What kind of Germany will be born? The French Anxiety); or the opinion polls conducted by *Le Figaro*, 1 October 1990, which found that half those asked said that the name they thought of when they thought of Germany was 'Hitler'; see also 'Bonds of suspicion' by Scott Sullivan, *Newsweek*, 30 April 1990; 'Le chauvinisme allemand' (German chauvinism) by Antoine-Pierre Mariano, *Le Figaro*, 5 February 1991. See also the following books: *La grande illusion* (The Great Illusion) by the prominent intellectual financier, Alain Minc (Grasset, Paris 1989) in which he argues that the unification of Germany will finish off the EC; finally *France-Allemagne: Le retour de Bismarck* (France and Germany: the return of Bismarck) by the editor of *L'Express*, Georges Valance, Flammarion, Paris 1990.

10. *Le Monde*, 27 March 1990.

11. See 'Le pari allemand de M. Mitterrand' (M. Mitterrand's German wager), *Le Monde*, 27 March 1990; Georges Valance, op. cit., pp. 24-25; 'A relationship in the balance', *The Economist*, 6 October 1990; 'Race to unification alarms French', *The Times*, 16 February 1990.

12. 'German unification is not on the agenda' declared Mitterrand in 1989, see *Figaro-Magazine*, 29 September 1990, p. 63.

13. 'La Semaine' by Christine Clerc, *Figaro-Magazine*, 29 September 1990.

14. *Le Fig-Eco* (Figaro Business Pages), 3 October 1990.

15. Ibid.

16. *Le Figaro*, 4 October 1990.

17. *Le Monde*, 9 October 1990.

18. *Le Monde*, 21 March 1990.

19. 'Le pari allemand de M. Mitterrand' (M. Mitterrand's German wager) in *Le Monde*, 27 March 1990; 'La teutomanie et le pari de Pascal' (Teutomania and Pascal's wager) by Serge-Christophe Kolm in *Le Monde*, 21 February 1990.

20. See e.g. 'France-Allemagne-Europe' by Thierry de Montbrial, *Le Figaro*, 12 December 1990.

21. See 'A relationship in the balance' in *The Economist*, 6 October 1990;

the same point is made a few months previously in 'A democratic way to European Unity' by William Cash, Bow Group, London, June 1990, p. 18.

22. *Figaro-Magazine*, 29 September 1990, p. 63.

23. Speech to the European Movement at UNESCO, 6 October 1990, Paris; see also Klaus Wagenbach (ed.), *Firma Frankreich* (France plc), Berlin 1989: 'the publicity made for Europe by France is just a bluff'.

24. 'Quelle politique etrangère?', *Le Monde*, 9 October 1990.

25. Arnulf Baring, Stuttgart 1988.

26. Helmut Plessner, Stuttgart 1959.

27. ed. Peter Longerich, Munich 1990.

28. Michael Sturmer, Berlin 1983; also *The Restless Great Power* by Thomas Nipperdey, Munich 1983.

29. Karl-Rudolf Korte in *Liberal* 4 (1974).

30. Ibid.

31. Werner Weidenfeld, *Der Deutsche Weg* (The German Way), Berlin 1990.

32. Weidenfeld, op. cit. p. 9.

33. Heinrich Heine, *Deutschland, Ein Wintermarchen* (Germany, a Winter's Tale), 1844, Caput VI, Verse 6.

34. *Zum Ewigen Frieden*, 1795.

35. *System des transzendentalen Idealismus* (System of transcendental Idealism), 1800.

36. Friedrich Nietzsche, 'Völker und Vaterländer' (Peoples and Fatherlands) in *Jenseits von Gut and Böse* (Beyond Good and Evil) 1885.

37. Arnulf Baring, *Unser neuer Gröenwahn: Deutschland zwischen Ost und West* (Our new Megalomania: Germany between East and West), Stuttgart 1989.

38. See John Laughland, 'The Thousand Year Reich', *The Spectator*, 21 June 1991; Noel Malcolm, 'Europe's Unholy Godfathers', *The Spectator*, 23 September 1989; see also Lady Diana Mosley, *Loved Ones*, 1990, especially the chapter on Sir Oswald Mosley, which mentions his desire to 'build Europe' and his magazine *The European*; for a full account of Nazi Europeanism, see *When Nazi dreams come true* by Robert Herztstein, Abacus, London 1982.

39. *Das innere Vaterland: Literarische Essays aus dem Exil* (The inner fatherland: literary essays from exile), ed. Martin-Gregor Dellin, Munchen 1986.

40. Official report at *Verhandlungen des deutschen Bundestags*, 1 Wahlperiode, Stenographische Berichte, Band 1, 18 Sitzung, 24 und 25 November 1949 (Bonn 1950) p. 525f. Note that this took place after the Western monetary reform and the Berlin airlift.

41. *Erinnerungen* (Memoirs) 1945-1953, Deutsche Verlagsanstalt, Stuttgart, 1965, p. 549f.

42. *Erinnerungen* (Memoirs) 1953-1955, op. cit., p. 301.

43. Cabinet meeting, 21 February 1951, see Hans-Peter Schwarz, 'Adenauer', Stuttgart, 1986, p. 836.

44. A secret memorandum from the British Ambassador in Berlin to the Prime Minister, Churchill, is quoted by Josef Fosschepoth in his *Adenauer und die deutsche Frage* (Adenauer and the German question), Gottingen 1988. Adenauer had confided to the Ambassador that he did not trust the Germans to make the right choice.

45. Quoted by Werner Weidenfeld, *Der Deutsche Weg*, op. cit., p. 149.

46. Baring makes this point in *Unser neuer Gröenwahn*, op. cit., pp. 67-68; as does Foschepoth in *Adenauer und die deutsche Frage*, op. cit., p. 22.

47. Foschepoth, op. cit., p. 20.

48. See Weidenfeld, op. cit., pp. 151-152.

49. The total level of subsidy was never revealed by the West German government and it took a number of different forms, making the sums difficult to add up. The most exhaustive investigation has estimated the total annual subsidy at DM 6 bn (£2 bn). This represents 60% of the cost of all German imports from OECD countries and 80% of imports from West Germany. Using the official East German figures for the economy, this represented 15% of 'produced national income' and therefore the real ratio is likely to be several multiples of this figure. See: 'Financial and material transfers between East and West Germany', by Jerzy Lisiecki, *Soviet Studies* Vol. 42, No. 3, July 1990, pp. 513-534. A dubious aspect of this was the West German government's policy of paying ransom money for political prisoners in East Germany. Genscher was also behind the policy of buying out Romanian Germans who wanted to emigrate from life under the Ceausescu dictatorship. The West Germans paid DM 8,000 per head for these emigrations to be permitted, leading the Romanian dictator to boast that his best exports were 'oil, Jews and Germans'.

50. Vertrag uber die Grundlagen der Beziehungen zwischen der Bundesrepublik Deutschland und der Deutschen Demokratischen Republik (Treaty on the Basis for Relations between the Federal Republic of Germany and the German Democratic Republic), 8 November 1972.

51. On France, see Michel Winock, *Nationalisme, antisémitisme et fascisme en France*, Paris 1990, Chapter 3, 'L'antiaméricanisme français'. Jack Lang, the long-standing Minister for Culture and Mitterrand's spokesman at the Elysée Palace, is known for his hatred of 'American cultural imperialism.' It is the common currency of discussion about the European Community in France that the closer integration of Europe will enable her better to pursue her interests against those of America and Japan.

52. Mikhail Gorbachev, *Perestroika: New Thinking for our Country and the Whole World*, p. 208.

53. Quoted by Foschepoth, op. cit., p. 9.

54. 'Europe in the 1990s', W.H. Smith Contemporary Papers, ed. Philip Ziegler.

55. Lecture to the Friedrich-Ebert-Stiftung in Washington, 29 May 1987, quoted by Baring, op. cit., p. 304f.

56. *Der Spiegel*, 24 August 1987. Helmut Schmidt expressed his resentment at this country's 'undesirably excessive dependence on the United States' in 'Einer unserer Brüder: Zum Besuch Erich Honeckers' (One of our Brothers: the Visit of Erich Honecker) in *Die Zeit*, 31 July 1987.

57. He made this remark twice in speeches in his home town, Halle, as East Germany was in turmoil at the end of 1989. Quoted by George Valance, *France-Allemagne: Le retour de Bismarck*, op. cit., p. 27.

58. See *The Guardian*, 7 May 1989, for example.

59. 'A Svengali on the defensive' by David Marsh, *Financial Times*, 28 January 1990.

60. Ernst Moritz Arndt, *Germanien und Europa,* 1803; Novalis, *Die Christenheit oder Europa* , 1799.

61. For an English translation of this work, see *Leibniz's political works*, ed. Patrick Riley. Leibniz discussed this idea with the French thinker Bossuet in letters written between 1691 and 1699. Leibniz is also credited with masterminding the Hanoverian Succession to the throne of England through his close friendship with the Electress Sophie. He discussed his desire for a united Christendom with her and his ideas were well known at the Hanoverian court. His correspondence with the English Ambassador, James Cresset, on the Hanoverian claim, as well as his undoubted acquaintance with the envoy, played an important role. See 'The Electress Sophia and the Hanoverian Succession' by Adolphus William Ward, Longmans, London, 1909, p. 319.

62. Quoted by A.J.P. Taylor, *Bismarck: The Man and Statesman.*

63. 'Is a strong Germany a cause for worry in a Europe which is growing together? Is it not rather a gain for the whole of Europe?', in Hans-Dietrich Genscher, 'Wir wollen ein europäisches Deutschland und nicht ein deutsches Europa' (We want a European Germany and not a German Europe), p. 37 in *Angst vor Deutschland* (Fear of Germany), ed. Ulrich Wickert, Hamburg 1990.

64. Thomas Hobbes, *Leviathan*, Part II, Chapter 17.

65. Werner Weidenfeld, *Der deutsche Weg*, Berlin 1989, p. 174.

66. Hagen Schulze, *Wir sind, was wir geworden sind* (We are what we have become), Munchen 1987, p. 113.

67. Noel Malcolm rightly draws attention to the near-fanaticism of the self-styled pro-Europeans in 'Lies, Damned Lies and Federasts' in *The Spectator*, 22 June 1991. See Noel Malcolm (again), 'The slings and arrows of Mr. Edward Heath', *The Spectator*, 29 June 1991.

68. Renate Fritsch-Bournazel, 'Confronting the German question: Germans on the East-West divide', Berg, Oxford, 1988, p. 21.

69. 'Wir wollen ein europäisches Deutschland und nicht ein deutsches Europa' in *Angst vor Deutschland*, ed. Wickert, op. cit., p. 322.

70. Ibid, p. 324. Or again, on the difficulties of achieving EMU, Genscher says, 'the tendency to think in terms of nation states must be overcome by a European attitude', as if it were only a matter of willpower. See his speech to the European Movement at UNESCO, Paris, 6 October 1990.

71. See 'The Thousand Year Reich' by John Laughland, *The Spectator*, 22 June 1991.

72. This is a great left-wing shibboleth. See Rudolf Bahro, 'Wahnsinn mit Methode' (Method in Madness), Berlin 1982, p. 69: 'This frontier between the two blocs and the concentration of destructive power on both sides of it – this is what in a crisis would turn our country, before any other in Europe, into a shooting range for the two superpowers. Because this is where the world divides between them, we are the ones in greatest danger...This is the common danger shared by both German states. They are united precisely in this point... so it is no accident that they now seem to be united in one Peace Movement.' See also W. Venohr (ed.), *Die deutsche Einheit kommt bestimmt* (German unity will definitely come) Bergison-Gladbach 1982, p. 6: 'Faced with visions of doom, Germans in both East and West talk of all imaginable prospects to come but one: the fact that the country in which they all live is the target of both military blocs; GERMANY, site of the Super-Holocaust to come.'

73. Remarks such as this: 'The ecological consciousness of the [US] government and people is not sufficiently enlightened' suggests an assumption of superior understanding. See 'Neue deutsche Fragen' (New German Questions) by Prof. Dr. Christian Hacke in *Frankfurter Allgemeine Zeitung*, 4 January 1991, p. 8.

74. See Genscher's speech to the Bundestag reported in *The Guardian Weekly*, 7 May 1989.

75. Interview in *Cologne Express*, 13 April 1990.

76. See *Federal Republic of Germany and EC Membership Evaluated*, edited by C.C. Schweitzer and D. Karsten, Pinter Publishers, London, 1990.

Chapter Six: Federalism

1. Sir Leon Brittan uses this tactic, e.g. interview on 'Today', BBC Radio 4, 2 April 1990.

2. Sir David Steel, among others, tries this one on, e.g. 'Call Nick Ross', BBC Radio 4, 18 June 1991. See letter to the *Daily Telegraph*, 7 October 1991, by W. Cash.

3. Michael Burgess, 'Can comparative federalism really be comparative?' in *Centralising and Decentralising Trends in Federal States*, ed. C. Lloyd Brown-John, 1988, p. 13.

4. Douglas Ashford, 'Democracy, Decentralisation and Decisions in Subnational Politics', Sage Professional Papers in Comparative Politics, Beverly Hills, 1976.

5. G.A. Almond and G.B. Powell, *Comparative Politics: Systems, Process and Policy*, 2nd ed., Boston 1978.

6. Rufus Davis, *The Federal Principle: A journey through time in search of a meaning*, Berkeley 1978.

7. Frank N. Trager, 'On Federalism' in *Why Federations Fail*, ed. Thomas Franck, New York 1968.

8. Theo Ohlinger, 'Austrian Federalism', Chapter XVII of ed. Lloyd Brown-John, op. cit., pp. 225-231.

9. See Table 1, p. 47 in Dale Krane, 'Evolutionary Patterns on Federal States' in ed. Lloyd Brown-John, op. cit., Chapter IV; or Table 119 of *Revenue Statistics of OECD Countries 1965-1989*, OECD, 1990.

10. Dale Krane, op. cit., p. 45.

11. Rejean Pelletier, 'Federalism and Upper Houses: Searching for a Solution' in ed. Lloyd Brown-John, op. cit., p. 63.

12. See Ernst Weibel, 'Swiss Federalism and its evolution in comparison with West Germany, Austria and Yugoslavia' in Lloyd Brown-John, op. cit., p. 205; Thomas Nipperdey, 'Föderalismus in der deutschen Geschichte' (Federalism in German History) in *Federalism: History and Current Significance of a Form of Government*, Martinus Hijhoff, The Hague, 1980, p. 172.

13. W. Weber, *Spannungen und Kräfte in westdeutschen Vergassungssystem*

(Tensions and Forces in the West German Constitutional System), Stuttgart 1951, p. 65.

14. Thomas Nipperdey, op. cit., pp. 167-168.

15. 'Germany recounts the cost', *The Economist*, 29 June 1991, p. 25.

16. Donald F. Kettl, *The Costs of Federalism*, ed. R.T. Golembiewski and Aaeron Wildarsky; see also David Caputo, 'Recent Domestic Policy in the U.S.' in ed. Lloyd Brown-John, op. cit., p. 172.

17. 'A Flawed Federalism', *International Herald Tribune/New York Times*, 9-10 February 1991.

18. F.C. von Flante, *Die Entwicklung der Schweiz zum Einheitsstaat*, 1877. For the last decades, see Ernst Weibel in Lloyd Brown-John, op. cit., p. 195 and Franz Lehner, 'The political economy of interlocked federalism: A comparative view of West Germany and Switzerland' in ed. Lloyd Brown-John, op. cit., p. 209.

19. Franz Lehner, op. cit., p. 211.

20. Donald Kettl in ed. Golembiewski et al, op. cit., p. 72.

21. Kettl, op. cit., p. 77.

22. 'America and Europe', *The Economist*, 23 March 1991, p. 24; 'The curse of checks and balances', *The Economist*, 13 October 1990, p. 14.

23. 'The American example Europe must avoid', by Janet Daley, *The Times*, 24 May 1989; Kettl, op. cit., p. 73.

24. For the weaknesses of the Senate, which is supposed to represent the States, see 'Bleak upper house', *The Economist*, 30 June 1990.

25. At the beginning of July 1991 there were 3 million unemployed out of a population of 16 million in the former East Germany. The then President of the Bundesbank, Karl-Otto Pöhl, used the word 'disaster' to describe the effects of monetary union with East Germany; see 'Pöhl says German monetary union proving a disaster', *Financial Times*, 20 May 1991; this outcome was predicted nine months beforehand by Mark Almond, 'Feeding a fledgling economy's almost insatiable appetite', *The Times*, 1 August 1990. See also 'And never the twain shall meet' by Anne McElvoy, *The Spectator*, 29 June 1991.

26. See Special Survey on Canada, *The Economist*, 29 June 1991.

27. Murray Forsyth, *Unions of States: The Theory and Practice of Confederation*, New York 1981, p. 167.

28. A. Stevens, *A Constitutional View of the late War between the States*, Philadelphia 1868.

29. Janet Daley, 'The American Model Europe Must Avoid', *The Times*, 24 May 1989.

30. Murray Forsyth, op. cit., p. 167.

31. Heinrich von Treitschke, 'Bund und Reich' (Federation and Empire) in *Preussische Jahrbucher* Vol. 2, 1876, p. 339.

32. See Treitschke's *Deutsche Geschichte im 19 Jahrhundert* (German History in the 19th Century).

33. See E. Zechlin, *Die deutsche Einheitsbewegung* (The German Unification Movement), Frankfurt, 1967, p. 83.

34. The American confederation of 1781 and the Dutch Union of 1579 were the products of wars waged against imperial powers and indeed the *Deutscher Bund* (German Federation) itself was primarily a defence union, with only one article in its constitution (Article 19) making provision for trade matters.

35. See 'La pensée economique allemande' (German economic thought) in *Le Monde*, 2 October 1990. List may have been influenced by that classic of economic totalitarianism, *Der geschlossene Handelstaat* (The closed trading state) by the idealist philosopher, Johann Gottlieb Fichte, published in 1800.

36. *Die Grundsätze der Realpolitik* (The Principles of Realpolitik, 2nd ed., 1869, pp. 26-27.

37. Murray Forsyth, *Unions of states*, op. cit., p. 172; Friedrich List, *Schriften* (Writings), Vol. VII, p. 471ff.

38. Murray Forsyth, op. cit., pp. 173-174. It is interesting to see the same ideas resurfacing under the Nazis, who believed that this kind of state capitalism was the secret of the power of the British Empire. See Paul Kluke, 'Die nationalsozialistische Europaideologie' (National-socialist Europe ideology) in *Vierteljaresschrift für Zeitgeschichte*, July 1955, Vol. 3. For the truth abut the lamentable economic reality of the Empire, see Corelli Barnett, *The Collapse of British Power*, 1972, especially Chapter 3.

39. See W.O. Henderson, *The Zollverein*, 1959, p. 96.

40. W. Fischer, 'The German Zollverein' in *Kyklos*, XIII, 1960, p. 80.

41. Murray Forsyth, op. cit., p. 167.

42. W. Fischer, op. cit., p. 80.

43. An exhaustive account is given by W.M. Freiherr von Bissing, 'Der deutsche Zollverein und die monetären Probleme' in *Schmollers Jahrbuch* 79 (1959), p. 199 ff.

44. Heinrich Triepel, 'Unitarismus und Föderalismus im Deutschen Reich' (Centralism and Federalism in the German Empire), Tübingen, 1906, p. 25.

45. See A.J.P. Taylor, *Bismarck, The Man and Statesman*, Hamish Hamilton, London, 1955, p. 99.

46. See Thomas Nipperdey, 'Föderalismus in der deutschen Geschichte' (Federalism in German History) in *Federalism: History and Current Significance of an Idea*, Martinus Nijhoff, The Hague, 1980, p. 142.

47. Murray Forsyth, op. cit., pp. 205-206.

48. Speech at the Franco-German colloquium at UNESCO, Paris, 6 October 1990: 'our position in the heart of Europe accords us greater responsibilities'.

49. See Heinrich Triepel, op. cit., passim. See also Nipperdey, op. cit., who says, 'the constitution contained national unitarian, federative, hegemonial, liberal and patrician anti-parliamentary principles', p. 145.

50. E.R. Huber, *Bewahrung und Wandlung* (Preservation and Change), Berlin 1975, p. 84.

51. Thomas Nipperdey, op. cit., p. 148.

52. Heinrich Triepel, op. cit., p. 111.

53. See Prof. Dr Graf Kielmansegg in *Frankfurter Allgemeine Zeitung*, 7 December 1990, 'Ohne Historisches Vorbild' (There is no historical model).

54. Th. Flathe, *Deutsche Reden* (German speeches) Vol. 2, Leipzig, 1894, p. 2.

55. See for example, 'La France veut-elle encore une agriculture?' (Does France still want to have an agricultural sector?), *Le Figaro*, 10 December 1990.

56. One could fill up a little scrapbook of anti-liberal, anti-American remarks by French Europhiles. Here are some examples: 'M. Delors invite le Parti

Socialiste a défendre le modèle européen de societé' (M. Delors asks the Socialist Party to defend the European model of society), *Le Monde*, 10 November 1990; 'Le capitalisme a-t-il produit Hitler?'(Did capitalism produce Hitler?) by Alain Besançon in *Le Figaro*, 28 September 1990, in which he rightly attacks President Mitterrand's remark that 'communism produced Stalin just as capitalism produced Hitler, Mussolini, Salzar and several others' (Hitler came to power on an explicitly anti-capitalist ticket); 'Le printemps de l'humanisme' (The springtime of humanism) by Jacques Delors, *Le Monde*, 16 May 1990; 'Delors warns against unfettered capitalism' by David Usborne, *Independent*, 7 July 1990; 'Le libéralisme à bout de souffle' in *Le Monde*, 27 March 1990, reporting on President Mitterrand's remark that liberalism (in the economic sense) is 'out of breath'.

57. 'Wir wollen ein europäisches Deutschland und nicht ein deutsches Europa' (We want a European Germany and not a German Europe) by Hans-Dietrich Genscher in *Angst vor Deutschland* (Fear of Germany), ed. Ulrich Wickert, Hoffman und Campe, Hamburg 1990, p. 319.

58. See Klaus Hildebrandt, *German Foreign Policy from Bismarck to Adenauer*. Both A.J.P. Taylor and the great German constitutional historian, E.R. Huber (whose history of the German constitutions spans a dozen volumes) make the point that Bismarck's Empire was parliamentary and the Reichstag became more and more the centre of political power. See Taylor, *Bismarck*, op. cit., p. 98, and Huber, 'Bewahrung und Wandlung', op. cit., p. 91. Thomas Nipperdey makes the same point in *Federalism in German History*, op. cit., p. 149.

59. See M.P. Fogerty, *Christian Democracy in Western Europe (1820-1953)*, 1957; K. Wedl, *Der Gedanke des Föderalismus in den Programmen politischer Parteien Deutschlands und Osterreichs* (The Concept of Federalism in the political programmes of Germany and Austria), 1969. The *Oxford English Dictionary* gives the first use as in the papal encyclical *Quadragesima Anno* in 1931, but Thomas Nipperdey refers to it as being a doctrine already current in pro-Austria, anti-Prussian Catholic social theory under Bismarck. See Thomas Nipperdey, 'Föderalismus in der deutschen Geschichte', op. cit., p. 147. For a good brief account of Christian Democracy and its long connection with European Federalism, see 'Europe's Christian Democrats' in *The Economist*, 17 March 1990.

60. Interview on 'Today', BBC Radio 4, 14 December 1990.

61. In evidence to the House of Commons Foreign Affairs Committee, 1989/90, 82-II, p. 31.

62. Quoted from Heide von Salis-Bilfinger, *Föderalismus und Verantwortung* (Federalism and Responsibility), Zurich, 1980, p. 134.

63. Lecture to the London School of Economics, 9 November 1990.

64. Lecture organised by *Le Monde*, 16 January 1990.

65. *Economic and Monetary Union*, published by the European Commission, op. cit., Section 3.1 'Principles, Objectives and Coherence'; see also Delors Report, paragraph 42, 'Parallelism'.

66. *One Market, One Money*, European Commission, Chapter 1, Section 1, p. 13.

67. This phrase has been used by Hjalte Rasmussen, 'On Law and Policy in the European Court of Justice'. See also the Bruges Group pamphlet by Gavin Smith, 'The European Court of Justice: Judges or Policy Makers?', Occasional Paper 10.

68. As Prof. T.C. Hartley makes clear in his *The Foundations of European Community Law*, 2nd ed., Oxford, 1988, p. 78.

69. 'Drowning in the law lake', *The Times*, 5 May 1989.

70. See 'Measuring up to high standards' by Andrew Fisher, *Financial Times*, 27 January 1989.

71. Evidence of the German position is abundant: 'Le chancelier Kohl veut hâter l'union politique européenne', *Le Monde*, 30 March 1990; 'Bonn initiative behind ambitious target' by David Marsh, *Financial Times*, 20 April 1990; 'Kohl urges increased role for European parliament' by David Marsh, *Financial Times*, 29 October 1990; 'Kohl calls for surrender of sovereignty' by Denise Clavelous, *The European*, 16-18 November 1990; 'Cardinal Differences' (between France and Germany), *The Economist*, 3 November 1990.

72. 'Pöhl calls for two-speed move to EMU', by Anatole Kaletsky, *The Times*, 10 November 1990; 'Pohl says Germany and its neighbours could create monetary union now' by David Buchan, *Financial Times*, 20 March 1991; this was in the same speech in which he called German monetary union a 'disaster'.

73. Michael Mertes, Personal Advisor to Chancellor Kohl, and Norbert Prill (also from the Federal Chancellor's office), in an article which they said represented their personal opinions: 'Das verhängnisvolle Irrtum eines Entweder/Oder: eine Vision für Europa' (The fateful mistake of saying either/or: a vision for Europe), *Frankfurter Allgemeine Zeitung*, 19 July 1989.

74. In the *Financial Times*, 20 March 1991, see note 72 above.

75. See 'Too many cooks spoil Italy's budget' by John Wyles, *Financial Times*, 7 January 1991.

76. See 'The Internal Market' by Hans-Eckart Scharrer in *Federal Republic of Germany and EC Membership Evaluated*, ed. Schweitzer and Karsten, op. cit., p. 11.

Chapter Seven: A Hall of Mirrors

1. Leader in the *Independent*, 25 September 1991.

2. Evidence given by Mr Garel-Jones (Minister of State at the Foreign Office and his adviser, Mr Anthony Jay, to the European Legislation Select Committee on Tuesday 23 July 1991, at paragraph 23.

3. David Gow in the *Guardian*, 20 September 1991.

4. Boris Johnson in the *Daily Telegraph*, 18 September 1991.

5. *Daily Telegraph*, 10 July 1991.

6. Hamish McRae in the *Independent*, 11 September 1991.

7. David Marsh, 'Germany gets the monetary jitters', *Financial Times*, 6 August 1991.

8. Appendix 4, 17 Report, Select Committee on the European Communities 'Political Union: Law Making Powers and Procedures' (HL Paper 80) Session

1990-91, 23 July 1991.

9. Christopher Tugendhat and William Wallace, *Options for British Foreign Policy in the 1990s*.

10. *Frankfurter Allgemeine Zeitung*, 10 September 1991.

11. *Sunday Telegraph*, 22 September 1991.

12. *Daily Telegraph*, 8 October 1991.

13. *Evening Standard*, 10 October 1991.